北京科技战略决策咨询中心资助项目

U0694908

京沪深科技创新中心功能评价研究

Functional Evaluation Study of Beijing–Shanghai–Shenzhen
Center of Science and Technology Innovation

张士运 等◎著

经济管理出版社
ECONOMY & MANAGEMENT PUBLISHING HOUSE

图书在版编目（CIP）数据

京沪深科技创新中心功能评价研究/张士运等著.—北京：经济管理出版社，
2019. 12

ISBN 978 - 7 - 5096 - 5350 - 0

Ⅰ.①京… Ⅱ.①张… Ⅲ.①科技中心—评价—研究报告—北京、上海、深圳
Ⅳ.①G322

中国版本图书馆 CIP 数据核字（2019）第 273500 号

组稿编辑：张巧梅
责任编辑：张巧梅
责任印制：黄章平
责任校对：张晓燕

出版发行：经济管理出版社
　　　　　（北京市海淀区北蜂窝 8 号中雅大厦 A 座 11 层 100038）
网　　址：www. E - mp. com. cn
电　　话：(010) 51915602
印　　刷：三河市延风印装有限公司
经　　销：新华书店
开　　本：720mm × 1000mm/16
印　　张：13. 5
字　　数：164 千字
版　　次：2019 年 12 月第 1 版　　2019 年 12 月第 1 次印刷
书　　号：ISBN 978 - 7 - 5096 - 5350 - 0
定　　价：129. 00 元

京沪深科技创新中心功能评价研究小组

组　长　张士运

成　员　王　健　庞立艳　姚常乐　王丽芳

　　　　李冬梅　吕　鑫　赵丹丹　李京玉

顾　问（按姓氏笔画排名）

王　军　国家统计局北京调查总队　　副总队长

石林芬　华中科技大学　　　　　　教　　授

玄兆辉　中国科学技术发展战略研究院　研　究　员

李石柱　北京市教育考试院　　　　　院　　长

何　平　国家统计局统计科学研究所　研　究　员

宋卫国　中国科技指标研究会　　　　秘　书　长

前　言

作为创新型国家建设的重要组成部分，科技创新中心是科技强国建设的核心依托。2014 年 2 月 26 日，习近平总书记在视察北京工作时，首次明确赋予北京建设全国科技创新中心的城市发展定位。2014 年 5 月，习近平总书记在上海视察工作时提出，上海要加快向具有全球影响力的科技创新中心进军。2017 年 7 月 1 日，习近平总书记视察香港时亲自见证国家发展改革委与粤港澳三地政府共同签署《深化粤港澳合作推进大湾区建设框架协议》，明确了粤港澳大湾区国际科技创新中心的定位，深圳作为粤港澳大湾区的核心城市之一，在引领科技创新中心建设中肩负着重任。

为科学测度和评价京沪深科技创新中心建设进程，研究小组在深入研究科技创新中心内涵和功能的基础上，以"集聚、原创、驱动、辐射、主导"五大功能为框架，以国内外权威指标体系为参考，以数据可靠性、可比性和连续性为基础，构建了由 5 个一级指标、20 个二级指标组成的科技创新中心功能评价指标体系。本书从横向和纵向两个维度进行实证对比研究，分析各自的相对优劣势和近 5 年的发展态势，系统反映京沪深三地科技创新中心建设的主要功能特征和所处的地位，是全面量化评价京沪深科技创新中心功能的综合评价报告。

在本书编写的过程中，得到了中国科学技术发展战略研究院、中国科技指标研究会、国家统计局统计科学研究所、华中科技大学等智库单位专家学者的热情帮助和悉心指导，谨致以诚挚的感谢。科技创新中心功能评价工作处于探索阶段，本书的内容和成果仅代表课题组的观点，不足之处恳请社会各界提出批评与建议，帮助我们不断改进和提升。我们衷心希望通过本书为社会提供一个认识京沪深科技创新中心状况的窗口。

目　录

第一章

理论基础

一、科技创新中心内涵

结合国内外相关研究和世界知名创新中心实践经验，我们认为应该从禀赋、功能和意义三个层面去深入挖掘和理解科技创新中心的内涵：科技创新中心是指高端创新资源集聚、创新文化氛围浓郁、原始创新能力突出、创新驱动效果明显、辐射引领能力强劲，是新思想、新知识、新技术、新产品、新业态和新模式的策源地，在科技创新体系中占据主导地位的城市或区域，是全国乃至全球科技创新的龙头和风向标，也是国家参与全球创新竞争的核心依托。

因此，科技创新中心应该拥有一批世界领先的知识和技术成果、一批杰出的科学家和企业家、一批具有国际影响力的大学及研究机构、一批具有国际竞争力的创新型企业，更应该拥有适宜于创新创业的社会环境、成熟的资本市场与先进的制度安排，进而能够代表世界最先进生产力，实现创新链与产业链的开放融合，引领科技进步和经济发展。科技创新中心不同于科学中心或技术研发中心，包含丰富的内涵和外延，具有重要的发展规律。

二、科技创新中心功能

结合国内外相关研究，科技创新中心发展应具有如下标志：一是能够集聚各类创新要素和有影响力的科研组织，吸引高素质人才和拥有发达的资本市场；二是拥有比较完整、适宜的创新链和产业链，在形成一批具有国际影响力的科技成果和创意的同时能迅速地实现产业化；三是拥有大量高成长、活力迸发和具有国际影响力的创新型企业，在若干产业领域具有领先水平；四是具有"宜居""宜业"的生活与商业环境和容忍失败、多元包容的文化氛围。围绕创新链、创新生态的角度，并从知识生产、应用和扩散视角分析，认为科技创新中心应具有如下五种功能：

（一）集聚功能

集聚功能把科技创新资源，包括人才、资本、研发与服务机构、企业等有机集合到一起。集聚功能是科技创新中心的基础，反映了创新投入，体现了创新要素的涵养与流动，为产业升级和经济转型发展提供要素支撑。集聚功能是形成良好创新生态系统的关键。通过强大的集聚功能为区域内创新创业提供了丰厚的要素基础，也是科创中心其他功能得以实现的先决条件。只有依托得天独厚的科教资源，吸引全球高端人才资源，占有丰厚的科技条件资源，拥有便捷高效的科技服务资源，以及一大批富有创新精神的科技企业资源，才可能成为科技创新引领者与创新创业的首选地。

集聚功能	科技创新资源有机集合，实现全球高端创新资源"聚集、聚合、聚变"	人才集聚、资本集聚、机构集聚……
原创功能	新思想、新知识、新技术、新产品和新模式的发源地	科学发现、发明专利、学术论文、技术标准、原创产品……
驱动功能	科技成果得以迅速应用和产业化，科技创新成为驱动经济社会发展的第一驱动功能	产学研密切协同，高技术产业发达，新兴业态频现……
辐射功能	区域科技创新对周边或者外部地区的发展带动力和综合影响力	知识溢出、技术溢出、产业带动、人才流动、项目合作……
主导功能	在全国乃至全球科技创新中居于主导地位，能够引领全国乃至全球科技创新	产业链主导、知识产权主导、资本主导……

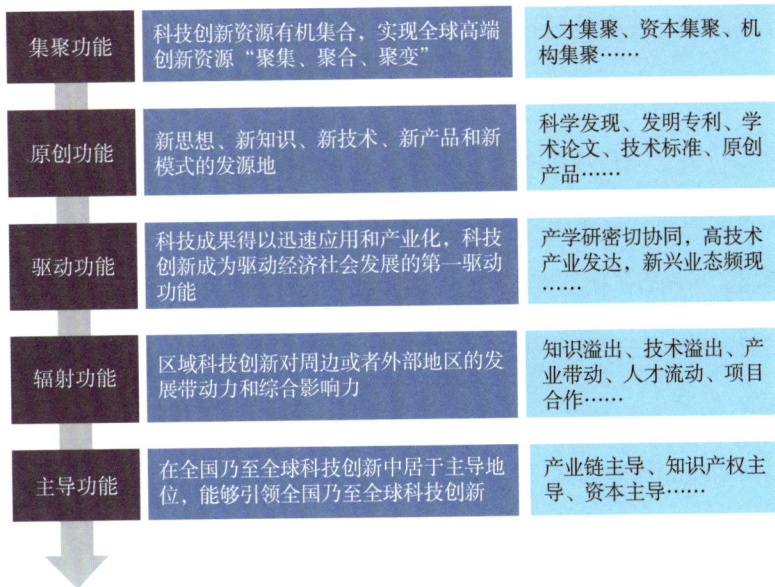

图 1-1 科技创新中心五大核心功能

创新资源的集聚和科技创新活动的空间分布，无论在全球尺度或地区尺度上，都是极度不平衡的，它们高度集中在全球少数地区或城市，犹如"钉子"般高高凸起，成为所在国家科技创新发展和科技综合实力的核心依托。

集聚功能的体现形式包括人、财、物、机构的集聚等方面。

（二）原创功能

原创功能是知识生产的表现。由于聚集一批勇于创新的人才和一流的高校、科研机构、创新型企业，必然形成集人才培养、知识创新和技术创新于一体，产生一系列原创成果，成为新思想、新知识、新技术、新产品和新模式的发源地。

原创功能是一个地区科学技术原始性创新的总体能力。包括科学的探知和发现，以及技术的理论形成和重大发明。原创功能的根本表现依赖于理论基础研究和应用基础研究的能力和水平，它不仅标志着一个国家和地区原始创新能力的强弱，也是国际大都市可持续发展的根本动力。美国学者 V. 布什曾指出："一个在新基础科学知识上依赖于其他国家的国家，它的工业进步将是缓慢的，它在世界贸易中的竞争地位将是虚弱的，不管它的机械技艺多么高明。"

原创功能的体现形式：基础研究经费投入、高水平论文的发表和引用、专利的发明和应用等。

（三）驱动功能

驱动功能是知识应用的表现。当今世界，科技成果转化周期越来越短，创新更迭和创新成果普及应用不断加快，呈现快鱼吃慢鱼态势，创新成果若无法实现快速转化，就无法转化为现实生产力，创新价值也就无法实现。为此，只有在创新生态中形成了每个角色都有将创新成果商业化的动力和环境（资本和服务）及保护各自利益的规则，实现了科技成果快速转移转化，从而通过产品创新、市场创新和管理创新带动产业变革，才是促进科技与经济社会深度融合发展的根本所在。

世界科技界有个共同难题，就是科技成果从实验室走进企业，变成社会所需要的产品。这段路程美欧科学家称之为"噩梦时代"，日本科学家将其称之为"死亡之谷"。许多科研成果只活在实验室与学术刊物里。

概括地讲，驱动功能就是指科技成果转化为现实生产力的能力。具体包括两个内涵：一是指科学研究与技术开发所产生的具有使用价值的科技成果的商业化应用和产业化；二是新知识、新思想、新理念、新设计和新创意等与科技紧密结合转化成现实生产力。也可以从三个层次上来理解驱动功能：从微观层面要关注技术成果的转化应用和产品开发；从中观层面要着力于科技资源集成、开放共享，产学研合力进行成果转化；从宏观层面要锐意改革创新，依靠科技进步、培育新兴产业、推动结构调整、转变发展方式。

驱动功能的主要表现形式：拥有比较完整、适宜的创新链和产业链，在形成一批具有国际影响力的科技成果和创意的同时能就地迅速实现产业化。基本实现方式包括：经济产出、高精尖产业结构、生产效率等。

（四）辐射功能

辐射功能是知识扩散的表现。由于创新中心拥有较多的原创成果、新知识、新技术和全球有影响力企业，从而与世界各地的创新形成比较优势，必然对全国乃至全球赋以强大的创新辐射功能。

科技创新辐射是指区域科技创新对周边或者外部地区发展的带动力和综合影响力，包括专利、人才、技术、市场等要素的流动和转移，以及科技创新思维方式等方面的传播，是区域之间保持联系、相互作用的基本运动形式，主要从辐射源和辐射流两方面来衡量。辐射源是指科技创新水平相对比较高的地区。辐射的媒介主要体现在交通条件、信息传播、人员流动、资金流动和技术转移等方面。辐射流则是指辐射源对外科技联系的能力。

作为科技创新中心，担负着通过科技成果和创新要素的高端辐射，引领带动科技创新和产业升级的使命。通过技术、资本、人才、信息、管理、政策等向周边地区和其他省区市乃至全球辐射溢出，通过绿色技术的转移带动全国城市精细化管理和生态文明建设，通过形成能够在全国范围内具有推广价值的创新观念、体制机制、创新环境和文化氛围，在全国乃至全球发挥示范引领作用，从而真正发挥科技创新引领者、高端产业策源地、生态建设示范城作用，辐射功能是发挥科技创新中心在全国乃至全球示范引领作用的关键，可以从知识技术溢出、人才流动、合作交流等维度来表征辐射功能。

知识技术溢出是指解释集聚、创新和区域增长的重要概念之一，克鲁格曼从核心竞争力培育的视角认为知识技术溢出是知识运用的结果，是知识管理的经济效应和表现形式。有学者研究认为，可从专利引用、创新产出、创新活动空间分布等不同维度研究知识技术溢出的存在性和可度量性，知识技术溢出成为影响空间集聚、创新与区域增长的重要因素，人才流动、研发合作、企业家创业、贸易投资等因素是知识技术溢出的重要机制。

辐射功能主要表现形式包括：知识溢出、技术流动、产业带动等方面。

（五）主导功能

主导功能是知识生产、应用和扩散的综合表现。在创新生态系统中形成了世界一流的创新企业和一流的原创成果，并占据价值链和创新链的高端，必然对全球科技创新和产业发展产生深远影响，从而最终形成支配和主导格局态势，成为国家创新战略的核心依托。主导功能是创新中心的终极表现，只有科技创新中心，才能具有统筹协调创新资源，引领创新方向的效能。

主导功能是对一个地区把握关键创新资源、掌握主动和掌控程度的衡量。作为科技创新中心必须要具备这种掌握全局的主导功能，需要强调的是这种主导绝非行政干预，恰恰是一种市场行为，在资源配置中能够发挥决定性的作用。

主导功能的主要表现包括：拥有大量高成长、活力迸发和国际影响力的创新型企业，在若干产业领域具有领先水平；通过知识产权、资本和产业链等牢牢掌握关键节点、关键要素、主动权、决策权和资源配置权等，进而获取产业链、价值链中的独特收益。

第二章

指数构建

科技创新中心功能评价是一项系统性工作，需要扎实的理论基础、合理的框架体系、科学的评价方法、可靠的基础数据。本书在科技创新中心五大功能理论的基础上，以国内外权威科技创新评价指标体系为参考，构建了科技创新中心功能评价指标体系。

一、构建思路

一是以科技创新中心"五大功能"理论为框架。结合科技创新中心的内涵与功能，以"集聚功能、原创功能、驱动功能、辐射功能、主导功能"为理论框架构建科技创新中心功能评价指标体系。其中，集聚功能表现为人、财、物、机构四方面的创新要素，原创功能表现在原创投入和原创产出两方面，驱动功能表现在产业优化和效率提升两方面，辐射功能表现为知识、技术和产业三方面，主导功能表现为技术主导和产业主导两方面。

二是以国内外权威指标体系为参考。充分借鉴硅谷指数、欧洲创新记分牌、全球创新指数等国际知名创新评价指数，以及国家创新指数、中国区域创新能力评价等国内权威创新评价体系的设计思想、指标选取、评价方法等。

三是以国家战略目标和国际对标为导向。指标体系中1/3指标设置思路来源于《"十三五"国家科技创新规划》《中长期发展规划》等文件中设定的科技发展目标，凸显科技创新中心的战略定位。在具体指标设置上，注重采用国际通用指标，如全社会研发经费支出占地区生产总值比重、劳动生产率等。

四是以数据可靠性、稳定性和连续性为基础。科技创新中心功能指数测算采用数据均来自权威资料和机构，包括《中国科技统计年鉴》《中国统计年鉴》等公开资料，中国科学技术信息研究所等部门以及国际权威榜单等，由此保证测算结果真实可靠。

二、指标体系

（一）选取原则

评价指标体系的评价结果是否客观准确，首先取决于各评价指标所含信息是否准确、全面。因此，选取什么指标评价科技创新中心功能是建立评价体系的核心，也是评价体系是否科学、客观、可行的关键。因此，在选择评价指标时遵循如下原则：

科学性原则：构建指标体系要从客观出发，运用合理的理论作为依据，同时在对数据进行处理和指数测算时采用科学方法，从而保证评价结果的真实可靠。

系统性原则：各指标之间具备一定的逻辑性，既能从不同侧面反映科技创新中心建设的状况，又能较为准确地反映"五大功能"之间的内在联系，共同构成一个有机统一体。指标体系的构建具有层次性,自上而下,从宏观到微观层层深入,形成一个不可分割的评价体系。

全面均衡原则: 指标体系能够覆盖科技创新中心的各个方面,全面考虑各要素之间的关系,各级指标要能对上一级指标进行全面反映。同时,还应注意指标层次、指标数量以及绝对量与相对量指标之间的关联等方面的均衡性。

可比性原则: 指标体系中的每一个指标必须反映被评对象的共同属性,且反映被评价对象属性中共同的内容,具有相同的计量范围、计量口径和计量方法。

可操作性原则: 选取的评价指标不仅应具有代表性,同时指标数据应易于采集,且信息可靠,易于从时间和空间上进行对比和评价。

(二)构建方法

通过借鉴国内外创新评价体系所采用的评价指标,并结合对集聚功能、原创功能、驱动功能、辐射功能和主导功能内涵的研究,科技创新中心功能评价采用树状评价指标体系,运用层次分析法由上而下逐层确定指标,最终形成二级指标体系,包括 5 项一级指标,20 项二级指标,详见表 2 – 1。

表 2 – 1 科技创新中心功能评价指标体系

	一级指标	二级指标
科技创新中心功能综合指数	集聚功能	万名从业人员 R&D 人员数
		R&D 经费投入强度
		高端仪器设备数量
		科研机构和高校数量

续表

一级指标		二级指标
科技创新中心功能综合指数	原创功能	入选全球高被引科学家数量
		基础研究经费占全社会研发经费比重
		SCI 论文数量
		万人发明专利拥有量
	驱动功能	高端产业就业人员占全社会就业人员比重
		新产品销售收入
		劳动生产率
		资本生产率
	辐射功能	异地合作科技论文数
		输出到异地技术交易成交额
		异地转让专利数占转让专利总数比重
		企业异地投资高新技术企业占比
	主导功能	入围全球研发投入 2500 强企业数量
		高技术产品出口额占商品出口额比重
		技术国际收入
		PCT 专利申请数

5 项一级指标，全面反映科技创新中心的核心功能。20 项二级指标，从投入—产出—绩效全链条多角度支撑科技创新中心五大功能。

1. 集聚功能指标

集聚功能把科技创新资源有机集合到一起，是科技创新中心的基础。集聚功能表现为四个方面——人、财、物和机构，具体指标设置为万名从业人员 R&D 人员数、R&D 经费投入强度、高端仪器设备数量、科研机构和高校数量。

2. 原创功能指标

原创功能是一个地区科学技术原始性创新的总体能力，既包括对原始创新的投入能力，也包括原始创新的产出能力，因此从投入和产出两个维度设置相关指标。投入包含人才和经费两方面，指标分别设置为入选全球高被引科学家数量、基础研究经费占全社会研发经费比重。产出反映在知识和技术两个方面，具体指标分别设置为 SCI 论文数量和万人发明专利拥有量。

3. 驱动功能指标

驱动功能是指科技成果转化为现实生产力，对地区经济社会发展产生积极影响，从而实现创新驱动发展的目标，包括产业结构优化、生产效率的提升等，具体指标设置上包括高端产业就业人员占全社会就业人员比重、新产品销售收入、劳动生产率和资本生产率。其中高端产业指知识密集型服务业和高技术制造业，从制造业和服务业两方面体现产业结构的提升。

4. 辐射功能指标

辐射功能是指区域科技创新对周边地区或者外部地区的发展带动力和综合影响力，主要表现在知识溢出、技术流动和产业带动三个方面，具体指标包括异地合作科技论文数、输出到异地技术交易成交额、异地转让专利数占转让专利总数比重、企业异地投资高新技术企业占比。

5. 主导功能指标

主导功能是科技创新中心的终极表现，只有充分发挥科技创新中心的主导功能，才能具有统筹协调创新资源，引领创新方向的效能。在指标体系中，表现在产业主导和技术主导两个方面，具体指标包括入围全球研发投入2500 强企业数量、高技术产品出口额占商品出口额比重、技术国际收入、PCT 专利申请数。

三、评价方法

（一）综合评价方法

多指标综合评价方法，就是把描述评价对象不同方面的多个指标的信息综合起来，并得到一个综合指标，由此对评价对象做一个整体上的评判，并进行横向或纵向比较。其基本思想是：要反映评价对象的全貌，就必须把多个单项指标组织起来，形成一个包含各个侧面的综合指标。从数学角度看，就是当选定 m 项评价指标 x_1，x_2，x_3，$\cdots$，x_m 时，对 n 个评价对象的运行状况进行分类或排序的问题。

科技创新中心功能评价采用线性综合评价模型：

$$y_i = \sum_{j=0}^{m} w_j x_{ij}$$

式中，x_{ij} 为第 i 个评价对象的第 j 项指标值，w_j 为评价指标 x_{ij} 的权重系数（$w_j \geqslant 0$，$\sum w_j = 1$），y_i 为第 i（$i=1$，2，$\cdots$，n）个被评价对象的综合评价值。

（二）指标权重设置

从线性综合评价模型的公式中可以看出，权重是影响综合评价结果的重要因素之一。在多指标的综合加权评价中，确定各项指标的权重是非常关键的环节，对各指标赋权的合理与否直接关系到分析的结论。

通过对国内外权威创新评价体系的研究，发现欧洲创新记分牌、全球创新指数、国家创新指数都采用等权重法对指标进行赋权。借鉴国际权威评价体系权重设置方法，并考虑到集聚功能、原创功能、驱动功能、辐射功能和主导功能对科技创新中心建设的作用是均等的，任何一项的缺失或弱化都会导致"木桶效应"，因此指标赋权采用等权重法。

（三）指标无量纲化

在多指标评价体系中，由于各评价指标的性质不同，通常具有不同的量纲和数量级。当各指标间的水平相差很大时，如果直接用原始指标值进行分析，就会突出数值较高的指标在综合分析中的作用，相对削弱数值水平较低指标的作用。因此，为了保证结果的可靠性，需要对原始指标数据进行标准化处理。

京沪深三地明确建设科技创新中心，因此选取三地开展实证评价，具体采用横向和纵向相结合的评价方法。考虑到科技创新中心建设是循序渐进的过程，因此在实证评价中，指数测算与评价采用定基比率法进行基础指标无量纲化处理。

第三章

总体评价

在国家和地方政府的支持下，京沪深三地科技创新中心建设进展明显。从科技创新中心功能评价结果看，京沪深科技创新中心功能综合指数均持续增长，集聚功能、原创功能、驱动功能、辐射功能和主导功能五项一级指数也表现出不同的增长态势，五大功能进一步强化。

一、功能综合指数增势稳定

2013～2017 年，京沪深科技创新中心功能综合指数整体均呈增长态势，2017 年分别达到 146.5、104.0 和 128.0，北京居首位，深圳和上海分居第二位和第三位。

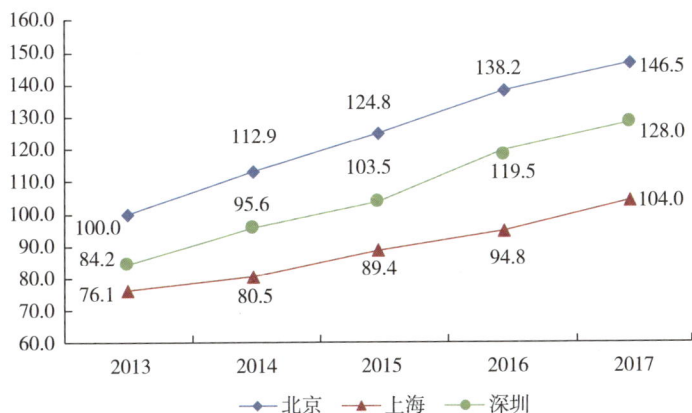

图 3-1 京沪深科技创新中心功能综合指数发展情况（2013～2017 年）

从三地差距看，2013～2015 年，三者差距呈扩大趋势，之后进入平行发展轨道，近两年差距保持平稳。2013～2017 年，京沪深科技创新中心功能综合指数分别提升 46.5、27.9 和 43.8。从 2017 年增长情况看，上海提升最为明显，指数较上年增长 9.2，明显高于深圳和北京的 8.5 和 8.3。

■ 二、五大功能指数各具特点

（一）从集聚功能看，北京资源禀赋雄厚

从五大功能指数看，北京在集聚功能指数上始终保持领先位置，且这种优势依旧在扩大，这与北京高度密集的科技创新资源，尤其是央属高校、科研院所等机构密切相关。

2017 年，京沪深集聚功能指数分别达到 128.7、71.4 和 50.6，沪深两地与北京存在明显差距，北京分别高出上海和深圳 57.3 和 78.1，具有绝对优势。从 2013～2017 年增长情况看，北京的领先优势越发明显，三地指数累计增幅分为 28.7、17.4 和 7.0。从具体指标看，北京的优势重点在于高端仪器设备资源、研发人员和高校院所的高度集中，上海在高端仪器设备方面相对深圳具有一定的优势，深圳则在研发人员强度上领先上海。科技创新中心集聚功能与先天资源禀赋高度相关，北京的资源优势是其他城市所无法比拟的，在短期内也无法赶超。

（二）从原创功能看，北京投入产出双高

高度的资源集聚必然带来大规模、高质量的创新产出。北京充分利用和发挥科技资源的有利条件，在科技创新产出方面也表现出强大的优势。

2017 年，京沪深原创功能指数分别达到 165.2、66.6 和 63.5，北京分别高出上海和深圳 98.6 和 101.7。从 2013～2017 年增长情况看，北京的优势持续扩大，三地指数累计增幅分别为 65.2、20.2 和 23.1。

从创新投入看，北京高水平科学家云集，高被引科学家数量长期位居全国首位，在基础研究方面的投入也处于全国领先水平，在科技发达省市中无论经费投入规模还是占全社会研发经费比重均居首位。从创新产出看，北京以论文为代表的知识创新产出和以发明专利为代表的技术创新产出成果丰富，SCI 论文数和万人发明专利拥有量都高居全国首位。

（三）从驱动功能看，深圳领跑态势稳定

2017 年，深圳驱动功能指数达到 184.1，较 2013 年提升 47.9，分别高于北京和上海 56.7 和 29.7。上海驱动功能指数为 154.4，高出北京 27.0。从发展趋势看，京沪深均表现出增长态势，北京、上海与深圳之间的差距呈扩大态势，北京与上海之间的差距则基本保持稳定。

从驱动因素分析，**高技术制造业是深圳驱动发展的强劲动力**。高技术制造业就业人员快速增长，2017 年高技术制造业就业人员数量占高端产业就业人员数量的 77.0%。同时深圳产品创新优势明显，2013～2017 年，新产品销售收入年均增长 15.7%，2017 年达到 1.2 万亿元，是北京的 2.9 倍，上海的 1.2 倍。**知识密集型服务业是北京驱动发展的重要推手**。知识密集型

服务业就业人员年均增长 7.8%，2017 年占高端产业就业人员总数的 90%
以上。

（四）从辐射功能看，北京带动效应突出

北京作为全国科技创新中心，是我国知识、技术的策源地，支撑自身发
展的同时，肩负着带动全国发展的重任。2017 年，北京辐射功能指数达到
116.9，位居首位，累计提升 16.9，分别高出上海和深圳 21.9 和 36.6。北
京辐射功能的优势主要在于知识的溢出以及输出技术整体规模较大，上海优
势在于较强的产业辐射能力，通过投资异地高新技术企业实现对其他区域科
技创新的带动作用，深圳优势则在于以专利为代表的知识产权转移活动的高
度活跃。

此外，从辐射地域来看，京沪深三地呈现出如下特征：

一是北京"飞地模式"：北京在呈现辐射带动全国的特征时，重点辐射
区域呈现出"飞地模式"的特征。**从论文合著看，**2017 年北京合著次数最
多的三省市是江苏、山东、广东，均在 2000 篇次以上，占合著次数前 10 位
省市总量的 35.5%。**从专利转移看，**2017 年北京转移专利最多的两省市是
江苏和广东，均在 400 件以上，占转移数量前 10 位省市总量的 38.1%。**从
企业投资看，**北京投资的前 10 名省份涉及东、中、西、东北各个区域，其
中湖南和上海最多，占比分别为 25.3% 和 12.0%，二者合计为 37.3%。属
于京津冀经济圈的天津和河北也进入前 10 位，二者合计占全部投资额的
16.3%。**从技术交易看，**2017 年北京流向外省市的技术合同成交额合计
2327.3 亿元，其中流向广东、四川两省最多，分别为 302.0 亿元和 279.3 亿
元，分别占流向外省市成交额的 13.0% 和 12.0%，合计占 1/4。

二是上海"近邻模式"：从论文合著看，2017 年上海论文合著省市中，江苏和浙江均位居前三位，合著次数在 2000 篇次以上，占合著次数前 10 位省市总量的 35.0%。**从专利转移看，**2017 年上海转移专利省市中，江苏和浙江分别位居第一位和第三位，分别超过 800 件和 400 件，占专利转移数量前 10 位省市总量的 47.7%。**从企业投资看，**上海以长江经济带为主，沿线省份占比高达 48.5%，其中地处长三角经济圈的江苏和浙江均进入前 5 位，合计占 34.3%，江苏更是以 26.7% 的比重稳居首位。**从风险投资看，**2017 年上海 VC/PE 投资机构对江浙皖三省总投资金额达到 233.5 亿元，江浙皖三省均进入接受上海 VC/PE 投资的前十名省市，充分体现了上海科技金融对长三角的辐射带动效应。

三是深圳"靶向模式"：从专利转移看，2017 年深圳向广东省外转移专利最多的省市为江苏，超过 400 件，专利转移数量占前 10 位省市总量的 22.7%，其他省市均在 250 件以下。**从企业投资看，**深圳投资地域非常集中，北京以近 2/3 的份额绝对领先，是深圳企业最青睐的投资区域。**从技术交易看，**2017 年深圳与上海地区技术交易额超越与广东省（除深圳）的交易额，成为排名第一的地区，合同数量 451 项，技术交易额 127.97 亿元，占输出到外地技术交易额的 56.9%。

（五）从主导功能看，深圳起点高增长快

深圳的主导功能指数领先优势明显，主要得益于深圳企业的国际化发展，着眼全球知识产权布局，尤其是华为、中兴、腾讯等龙头企业的带动作用非常突出。

深圳主导功能指数以 2013 年的 125.1 为起点，至 2017 年达到 261.6，

分别高于北京和上海 167.5 和 128.7，五年间累计增幅 136.5，北京和上海累计增幅分别为 94.1 和 62.2。从三者之间差距看，北京和上海与深圳之间的差距整体呈现扩大态势。

从实现主导功能的路径来看，京沪深三地呈现如下特征：

一是北京以央企为主对全球进行创新布局。在京央企是首都科技创新的重要载体，为北京建设全国科技创新中心贡献了重要力量。2017 年北京入围全球研发 2500 强榜单的企业中，排名前 10 位的企业除百度和联想外均为央企，且这 8 家央企的研发经费总量占北京全部入围 2500 强企业总量的 47.9%。同时，中央企业在高铁、特高压及智能电网等科技含量较高的领域占领部分国际科技制高点，获得了世界技术发展趋势的引领地位。

二是上海以外向型创新经济为主强化全球资源配置。上海作为中国大陆首个自贸区所在地，长期以来经济发展得益于外向型经济的带动，具有进出口商品总额高、技术国际收入高等明显特征。2017 年上海高技术产品出口额占商品出口额的比重为 48.6%，分别高于北京和深圳 5.8 个百分点和 5.2 个百分点。上海 2017 年实现技术国际收入 156.2 亿美元，分别是北京和深圳的 1.8 倍和 2.6 倍。

三是深圳以 PCT 实现全球知识产权布局。深圳主导功能指数起点高、增长快的特点突出，其首要推动因素是 PCT 专利申请量的高速增长。2017 年，PCT 专利申请量达 20457 件，占全国 PCT 申请总量的 41.9%，2013 ~ 2017 年年均增长 19.4%，仅华为一家企业 PCT 申请量就达到 4024 件，接近北京申请总量的 80%，是上海总量的 1.9 倍。

三、主要结论

实证评价结果显示，京沪深三地科技创新中心功能都在不断地发展和提升，科技创新中心功能综合指数都有较大增长。从功能综合指数看，北京居首位，近两年上海、深圳与北京的差距基本保持平稳，五大功能指数凸显三地不同优劣势和发展模式：

北京的集聚、原创、辐射三大功能指数排在首位，主导功能指数排在第二位、驱动功能指数排在第三位，呈现以高校院所为主导的技术驱动发展模式。北京先天禀赋优势明显，高校院所资源发达，科技成果丰富，是全国科技创新资源最集中的地区，也是全国知识、技术的策源地，向全国各地源源不断输出知识和技术成果，形成辐射引领全国的格局，担负起了全国科技创新中心的重要使命，体现了首都特色。驱动功能和主导功能相对短板，产业发展动能和全球创新影响力有待进一步提高。

上海的集聚、原创、驱动和辐射四项功能指数位居第二，主导功能指数位居第三，呈现以传统产业和高技术产业（新经济）并存的混合经济发展模式。上海整体发展较为均衡，且协调性较好。其中，集聚功能方面，上海在高端仪器设备、科学研究机构等方面都优于深圳，次于北京。原创功能方面，高水平科学家、基础研究经费投入、高水平论文产出三个方面优于深圳，次于北京。驱动功能方面，上海在资本生产率及新产品产出方面均优于北京，次于深圳。辐射功能方面，上海的产业辐射能力具有明显优势，带动其辐射功能指数持续稳定增长。主导功能方面，上海在高技术产品出口和技术国际收入两方面具有优势。值得关注的是，上海传统产业转型任务较重、高技术发展冲力仍待提升，以 PCT 为代表的知识产权主导是努力的重点方向。

深圳的驱动、主导两大功能指数排在首位，集聚、原创、辐射三大功能指数排在第三位，呈现以高技术产业（新经济）为特征的创新发展模式。深圳驱动功能指数的快速发展主要得益于劳动生产率的不断提升，以及新产品产出带来的经济效益，在产业发展方面，制造业的结构也不断优化提升，高技术所占比重不断增长。主导功能领先的关键因素是其企业全球专利布局的快速发展，尤其是华为、中兴等龙头企业的带动作用十分突出。深圳高技术发展动力强劲、传统产业转型任务不重、产业发展外向型明显，但科技资源不丰沛，对周边辐射作用仍须进一步提升，是值得重点关注解决的问题。

第四章

集聚功能评价

集聚功能把科技创新资源，包括人才、资本、研发与服务机构等有机集合到一起。集聚功能使城市实现全球高端创新资源的"聚集、聚合、聚变"，是形成良好创新生态系统的关键，也是建设科技创新中心的基础。

一、总体情况

集聚功能指数重点包括人、财、物和机构四个方面的指标。从评价结果看，北京在科技人力资源、研发经费投入、高端科研仪器设备和高校院所数量方面都具有绝对领先优势。上海、深圳 R&D 经费投入强度稳步增长，深圳在研发人才强度方面与北京接近，且 2015 年超过北京，具有一定优势。

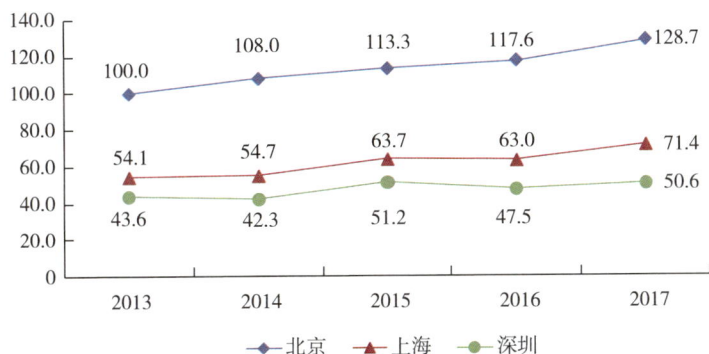

图 4-1　京沪深集聚功能指数发展趋势（2013~2017 年）

从具体指数来看，北京位居第一，上海位居第二，深圳位居第三。2013～2017年，北京集聚功能指数从100上升至128.7，累计提升28.7，上海集聚功能指数累计提升17.3，深圳集聚功能指数累计提升7.0。

二、具体分析

（一）北京研发人才规模强度领先

人才是创新活动的根本，是一个国家或地区的竞争之本、转型之要、动力之源。R&D人员是创新最为重要的人力资源之一，是指参与研究与试验发展项目研究、管理和辅助工作的人员，包括项目（课题）组人员、科技行政管理人员和直接为项目（课题）活动提供服务的辅助人员。万名从业人员R&D人员是反映相对就业规模创新人力资源状况的指标。

从R&D人员总量来看，近5年北京均高于上海和深圳。2017年，北京R&D人员为27.0万人年，深圳以19.6万人年位居第二，上海为18.3万人年。从R&D人员增长情况看，北京近5年年均增速为2.7%，上海为2.6%，深圳为4.4%。

从万名从业人员R&D人员数来看，近5年北京和深圳数值接近，且交替领先，均高于上海。从近5年年均增速来看，北京为4.3%，上海为2.0%，深圳为3.2%。北京的科技创新人力资源水平保持了相对较快的增长，说明北京的科技人力资源储备非常充沛，为科技创新活动奠定了良好的基础。

万人年

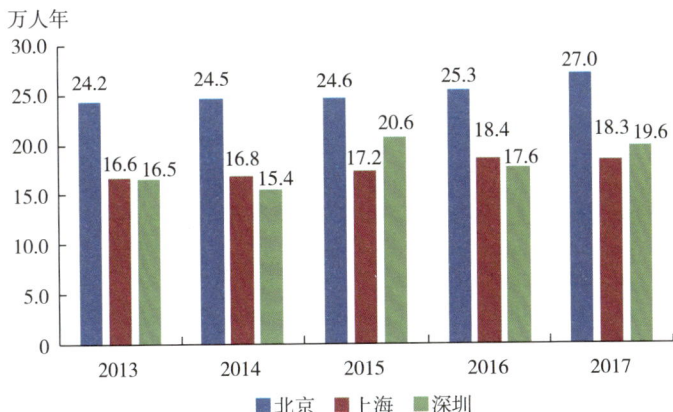

图 4-2　京沪深 R&D 人员总量发展趋势（2013～2017 年）

人年/万人

图 4-3　京沪深万名从业人员 R&D 人员数（2013～2017 年）

（二）北京研发投入强度保持高位

全社会 R&D 经费支出占地区生产总值比重是国际通用反映创新投入的指标，能够较好地评价一个地区科技创新能力和水平。北京 R&D 经费投入强度始终保持全国第一，2013 年以来稳定在 5.5% 以上，2017 年达到 5.64%，高于深圳 1.3 个百分点，高于上海 1.64 个百分点。从 2013～2017

年发展变化来看，北京 R&D 经费投入强度呈下降趋势，上海、深圳则稳步提升。近年来，上海围绕科创中心建设着力提升科技创新中心策源能力，2017 年 R&D 经费居全国第六位，年均增长 11.6%。深圳在创新上不断发力，研发投入持续增加，R&D 经费年均增长 14.5%。

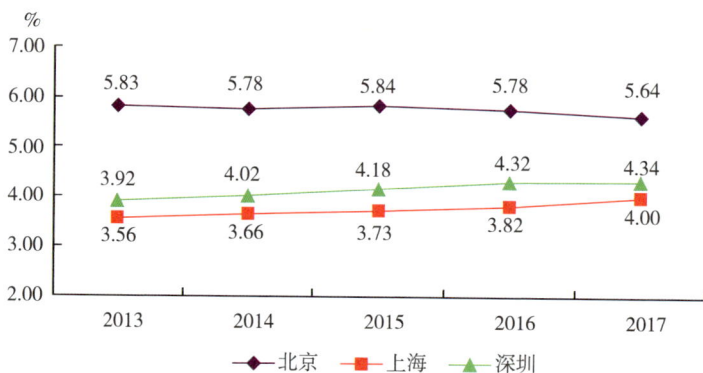

图 4 - 4　京沪深 **R&D** 经费内部支出占地区生产总值比重情况（**2013 ~ 2017 年**）

（三）北京高端仪器设备资源丰富

高端仪器设备数量反映了科研人员所拥有的科研物质条件，物质条件越丰厚，越能产生更多的创新成果，也能激发科研人员的创新积极性。北京地区拥有中科院、北大、清华等众多中央大院大所和高校，科技资源得天独厚。近 5 年来，高端仪器设备数量明显领先于上海和深圳，且呈现稳步上升的态势。2017 年，北京地区拥有高端仪器设备 795 台（套），分别是上海和深圳的 1.9 倍和 18.9 倍。

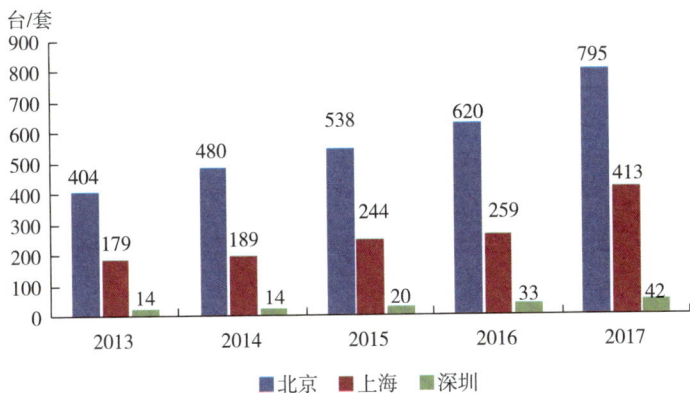

图 4 – 5 京沪深高端仪器设备数量（2013 ~ 2017 年）

（四）北京科学研究机构高度聚集

科研机构和高校是我国创新体系的重要组成部分，承担着科学研究的重任，其数量能够反映区域科学研究资源的聚集程度。2013 ~ 2017 年，北京科研院所和高校数量高于上海和深圳位列第一，始终保持在 460 家以上，是上海的 2 倍以上，深圳的 25 倍以上。上海位列第二，基本保持在 200 家左右。深圳位列第三，差距较大，但这类资源优势是长时间积淀的结果，在短时间内很难突破。

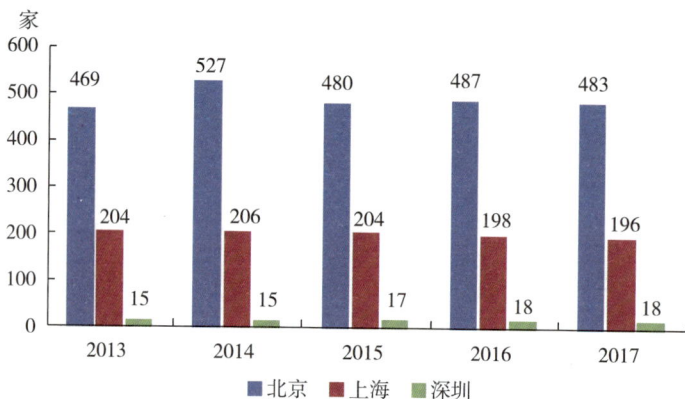

图4－6 京沪深科研机构和高校数量（2013～2017年）

三、小结

通过以上分析，在集聚功能方面，北京具备绝对优势，始终处于领先位置，上海和深圳也各具特点。

北京在集聚功能方面的优势与其特殊位置相关，大量央属高校院所的集聚带来了无法比拟的资源优势，在人、财、物方面都高度聚集，不但科技资源丰厚，而且人才与资金相对强度也领先。值得注意的是，每万名从业人员R&D人员数方面的优势正在逐渐减弱，甚至可能被赶超，在当前激烈的城市之间的人才竞争中，在集聚全球高端人才的同时也应注重吸引基层研发人才。

上海科技资源排第二位，在高端仪器设备拥有量以及高校院所数量方面仅次于北京，较深圳具备一定的优势。在研发人才强度和研发经费投入强度方面，人才和资金强度最低，万名从业人员 R&D 人员数近两年来在下降，与深圳、北京相比还有提升空间。

深圳人均研发投入和研发人才强度高于上海，万名从业人员 R&D 人员数上与北京接近，具有相对优势，在研发投入强度上仅次于北京，而且近年来深圳在创新上不断发力，研发投入持续增加，年均增长率高于北京和上海。深圳科技基础条件薄弱，在高端仪器设备数量、高校院所数量方面还存在较大的差距。

第五章

原创功能评价

原创功能是一个地区科学技术原始性创新的总体能力，是增强创新驱动源头供给的基础，是世界科技竞争的制高点，它不仅标志着一个国家和地区原始创新能力的强弱，也是国际大都市可持续发展的根本动力。

一、总体情况

原创功能指标重点包括原创投入、知识创新、技术创新等方面。从评价结果看，北京在原创投入、知识创新和技术创新方面均具有较强优势，随着全国科技创新中心建设工作的深入推进，北京作为原始创新策源地的位势更加巩固。2013～2017 年，北京原创功能指数从 100 上升至 165.2，累计提升65.2，5 年来北京科技创新中心的原创能力得到了较大提升。

图 5 - 1　京沪深原创功能指数发展趋势（2013～2017 年）

从京沪深评价结果对比看，北京原创功能居京沪深首位，且领先优势显著。2013～2017 年，北京与上海、深圳原创功能指数差距逐渐拉大，2017 年差值分别达到 98.6 和 101.7。

二、具体分析

（一）北京高被引科学家优势明显

入选"全球高被引科学家"名单，意味着该学者在其研究领域具有世界级影响力，其科研成果为该领域发展做出了较大贡献。近年来，北京以引进和培育高端人才为抓手，积极打造原始创新人才高地。2013～2017 年，北京入选全球高被引科学家的人数年均增长 12.3%，2017 年达到 94 人，是上海的 7.2 倍，深圳的 23.5 倍。

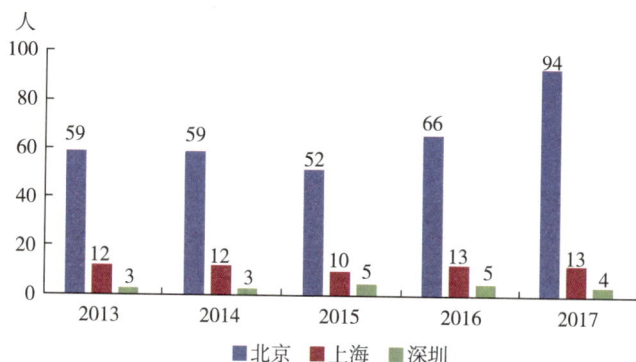

图 5-2 京沪深入选全球高被引科学家数量情况（2013～2017 年）

从入选名单分析看，科研实力较强的科研机构和双一流高校是全球高被引科学家的主要依托单位。北京凭借中科院在京院所较多和北京大学、清华大学的强劲优势，入选全球高被引科学家数量不断增长。上海复旦大学、上海交通大学虽表现不俗，但与北京相比仍有较大差距。深圳重点依托深圳大学、南方科技大学等非双一流高校，差距较大。

（二）北京基础研究投入领跑沪深

基础研究是原始创新的根基，也是产品和装备升级的支撑，体现了面向科学前沿的原始创新能力。2013～2017年，北京基础研究经费保持高速增长，由2013年的137.2亿元迅速提升至2017年的232.4亿元，年均增长14.1%。与上海、深圳相比，北京是创新链前端的"领跑者"。2017年，北京基础研究经费支出是上海的2.5倍、深圳的7.6倍。北京基础研究形成的重大原创科技成果，为突破重大尖端技术提升自主创新能力发挥了重要作用，已成为国家原始创新的核心力量。

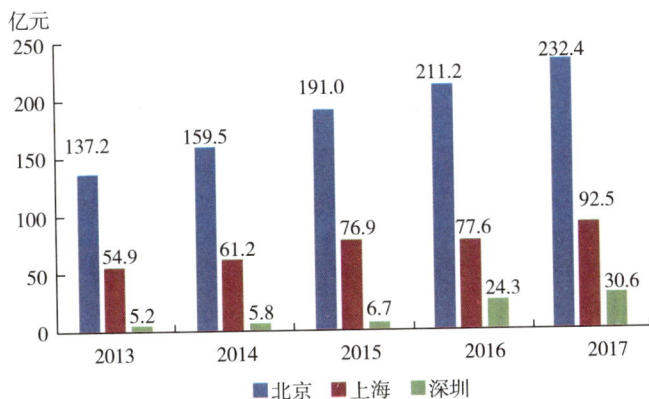

图5-3　京沪深基础研究经费支出情况（2013～2017年）

基础研究经费占全社会研发经费比重是国际通用反映原始创新能力的指标。2013～2017年，北京基础研究经费占全社会研发经费比重由11.6%上升至14.7%，累计提升3.1个百分点。远高于上海和深圳同期比例，北京在成为国家自主创新重要源头和全球原始创新主要策源地的道路上始终走在前列。

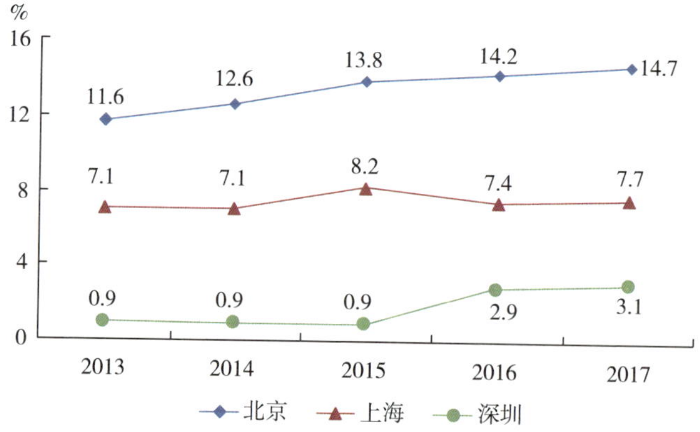

图5-4 京沪深基础研究经费占全社会研发经费比重情况（2013～2017年）

（三）北京知识创新产出能力居首

知识创新是科技创新的上游环节，科技论文作为知识创新成果，是原始创新水平和能力的重要体现。SCI收录论文数作为测度知识创新水平的重要指标，直接反映了原始创新能力。2017年北京发表SCI论文5.2万篇，是上海的1.9倍、深圳的17.3倍。2013～2017年，北京发表SCI论文数量年均增速为8.9%，高于上海（8.2%）0.7个百分点，低于深圳（27.6%）18.7个百分点。

万篇

图 5 – 5 京沪深发表 SCI 论文数量情况（2013 ~ 2017 年）

（四）北京技术创新产出快速增长

发明专利拥有量是体现技术创新实力的一个重要标志，是体现创新发展的重要指标。2017 年，北京发明专利拥有量达到 20.5 万件，是上海、深圳发明专利拥有量的 2 倍。2013 ~ 2017 年，北京发明专利拥有量年均增长 24.6%，分别比上海（20.1%）高出 4.5 个百分点、比深圳（14.6%）高出 10.0 个百分点。

万件

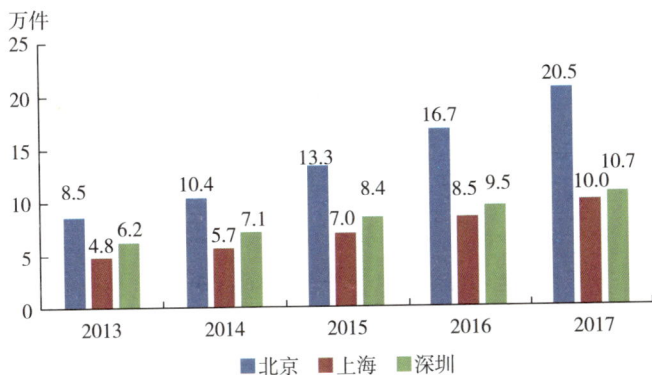

图 5 – 6 京沪深发明专利拥有量情况（2013 ~ 2017 年）

万人发明专利拥有量是国际通用指标，体现一个国家或地区技术创新产出能力。2013～2017 年，北京万人发明专利拥有量快速发展，年均增长 23.7%，高于上海（20.0%）3.7 个百分点、深圳（9.8%）13.9 个百分点。2017 年首次超越深圳，达到 94.6 件/万人。与上海相比，北京发明专利拥有量持续保持在上海的 2 倍以上，且差距呈逐步拉大趋势。

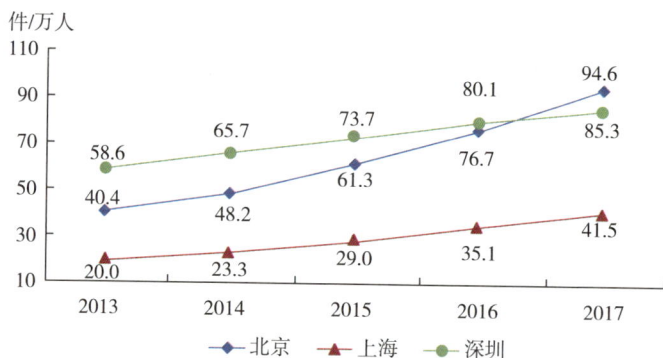

图 5 - 7　京沪深万人发明专利拥有量情况 （2013～2017 年）

三、小结

上述分析表明，在原创功能方面，北京表现出较强的优势，上海和深圳各具特点。

北京高端人才、基础研究投入、知识创新产出远高于沪深且增长趋势明显；万人发明专利拥有量在 2017 年超越深圳，实现全面领先，是原创投入、知识创新、技术创新的"排头兵"。

上海高端人才、基础研究投入、知识创新产出排名第二，其中基础研究经费占全社会研发经费比重在 2015 年以后呈现下降趋势。专利产出最低，在技术创新方面仍需努力，未来可充分挖掘潜能，激发和释放发展新动能，提升区域技术创新水平。

深圳万人发明专利拥有量在京沪深中排名第二，入选全球高被引科学家数量、基础研究经费投入、SCI 论文数量均居京沪深第三位，尽管 2015 年以后基础研究经费占全社会研发经费比重快速增长，但仍处于末位。未来需进一步加大原创投入和高端人才吸引与培育力度，创造更多的科学研究原创成果。

第六章

驱动功能评价

驱动发展是科技创新中心发展的核心动力，是促进科技与经济社会深度融合发展的根本所在，是实现产业变革和驱动社会发展的基础，是实现高质量发展的重要引擎，是塑造更多依靠创新驱动、更多发挥先发优势实现引领型发展的保障。

一、总体情况

驱动功能重点反映在产业结构优化和效率提升两个方面。从评价结果看，深圳驱动功能领先优势显著，近 5 年稳居京沪深三地首位，上海、北京分别位于第二位和第三位。2017 年深圳驱动功能指数为 184.1，分别高于北京的 56.7 和上海的 29.7。北京驱动优势集中在服务业结构优化升级方面，上海优势在于产品创新与资本产出效率两方面，深圳在产品创新效益、制造业结构提升、劳动产出效率与资本产出效率等方面均展现出较强优势。

从发展趋势看，京沪深驱动功能指数均呈现稳步增长态势。深圳增幅居京沪深之首。2013 ~ 2017 年，深圳驱动功能指数提高 47.9，增幅分别高于北京的 20.5 和上海的 19.0。北京、上海与深圳之间的差距逐年扩大，北京与上海之间差距基本稳定。

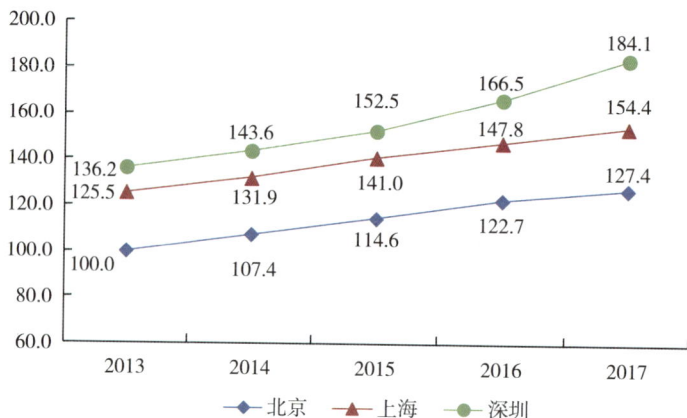

图6-1 京沪深驱动功能指数发展趋势（2013~2017年）

二、具体分析

（一）北京高端产业发展极具潜力

高端产业包括以高科技含量、高附加值为特征的知识密集型服务业和高技术制造业，从制造业和服务业两方面体现产业结构提升。北京高端产业就业人员在规模与增速方面均具有明显优势。2017年北京高端产业就业人员达317.5万人，是上海的1.6倍，深圳的1.5倍，2013~2017年，高端产业就业人员数量年均增速为6.7%，高出上海4.9个百分点和深圳3.7个百分点，高端产业人才的快速增长为高端产业发展提供了有力支撑。

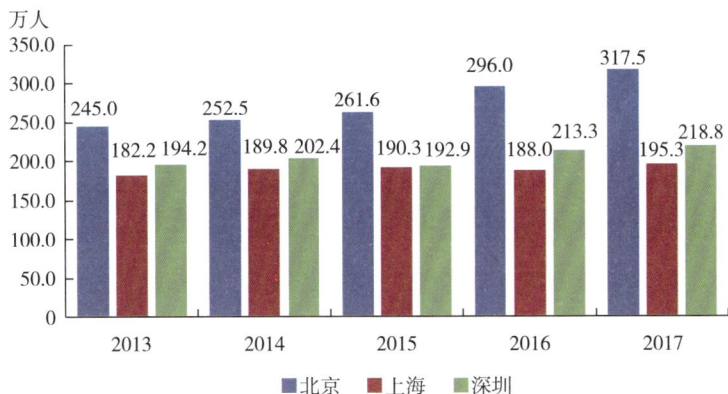

图 6 - 2　京沪深高端产业就业人员情况（2013～2017 年）

高端产业就业人员占全社会就业人员比重可以反映创新对产业结构的优化以及创新对就业的影响。北京高端产业就业人员占全社会就业人员比重自2015 年超过深圳后，近两年一直领先上海和深圳，2017 年为 25.5%，与2013 年相比提高了 7.0 个百分点，即每 4 个就业人员中就有 1 个人从事高端产业，分别高出上海 11.3 个百分点和深圳 2.3 个百分点。

图 6 - 3　京沪深高端产业就业人员占全社会就业人员比重情况（2013～2017 年）

（二）深圳产品创新产出稳居首位

新产品是创新最直接的产物之一，也是创新活动在市场中活跃度的反映。新产品销售收入的增长反映出供给侧结构的不断优化，以及经济发展质量的提升。2013～2017 年，深圳新产品销售收入年均增长 15.7% ，2017 年达到 1.2 万亿元，是北京的 2.9 倍，上海的 1.2 倍。上海、北京新产品销售收入分别位居京沪深第二和第三，北京新产品发展相对迟缓，新产品销售收入年均增长仅 2.9% 。

图 6-4 京沪深新产品销售收入情况（2013～2017 年）

（三）深圳劳动产出效率优势突出

劳动生产率是评价经济发展质量的综合性指标，从劳动节约的角度反映经济发展方式的转变，为生产总值与就业人员数之比。深圳劳动产出效率优势突出，2017 年劳动生产率为 23.8 万元/人，分别高出北京 1.3 万元/人和上海 1.5 万元/人。北京劳动生产率与深圳相比略有差距，近两年增速明显放缓。

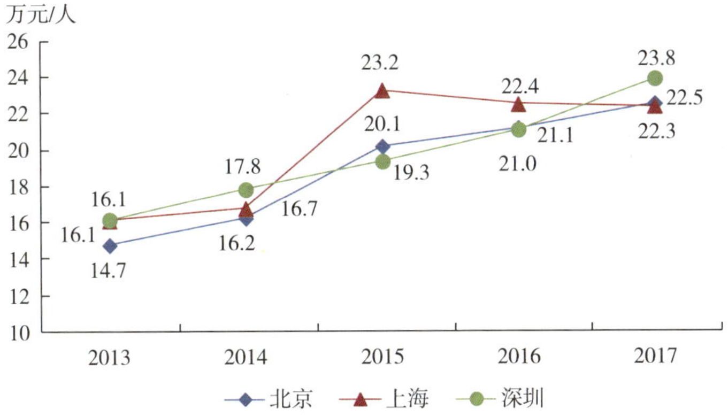

万元/人

图 6 – 5　京沪深劳动生产率对比情况（2013～2017 年）

（四）深圳资本产出效率稳居第一

资本生产率反映的是资本投入与经济产出之间的关系，是衡量单位资本产出能力的指标。深圳资本生产率虽整体呈现下降趋势，但始终保持领先位置，2017 年为 0.42 万元/万元，分别高出北京 0.04 万元/万元和上海 0.02 万元/万元。上海资本生产率呈现小幅增长，北京缓慢增长，与上海和深圳相比仍存在一定的差距。

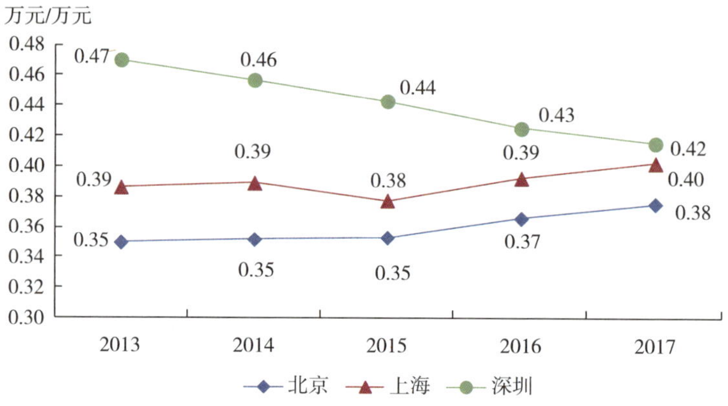

图 6 – 6   京沪深资本生产率对比情况（2013～2017 年）

三、小结

通过以上分析，在驱动功能方面，京沪深三地分别在不同方面呈现优势。

北京在发展以服务业为主导的高端产业方面具有相对优势，高端产业就业人员规模、增速以及占全社会就业人员比重等均高于上海和深圳，表现出较大发展后劲。在新产品开发和资本产出效率两方面仍需努力。

上海在产品创新、资本产出效率等方面居京沪深中间位置，与北京相比具有优势，但低于深圳。在高端产业、劳动生产效率等方面与北京和深圳仍存有差距，高端产业就业人员占全社会就业人员比重呈现下降趋势，需进一步提升。

深圳高端产业实力和发展效率突出，在产品创新、劳动和资本产出效率等方面体现了较强优势，新产品销售收入、劳动生产率和资本生产率均高于北京和上海。资本生产率呈现下降（边际递减）趋势，在高端服务业发展方面还有较大的提升空间。

第七章

辐射功能评价

辐射功能是指区域科技创新对周边或者外部地区发展的带动力和综合影响力，通过技术、资本、人才、信息、管理、政策等向周边地区和其他省区市乃至全球辐射溢出，是区域之间保持联系、相互作用的重要保障，是发挥科技创新中心在全国乃至全球示范引领作用的关键。

一、总体情况

辐射功能包括知识溢出、技术流动和产业带动三方面。从评价结果看，2017 年，北京辐射功能指数达到 116.9，位居首位，分别高出上海和深圳22.0 和 36.6。从指数发展情况看，京沪深辐射功能指数整体均呈上升态势，5 年间累计增幅分别为 16.9、11.3 和 4.4。

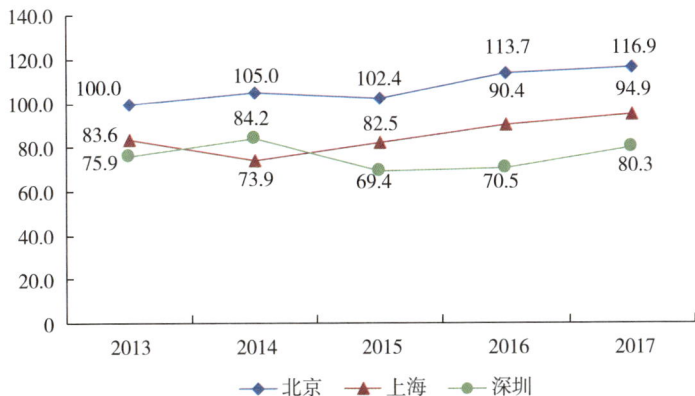

图 7 – 1 京沪深辐射功能指数发展趋势（2013～2017 年）

从具体指标看，三地各具优势，北京辐射功能优势主要在于知识溢出以及输出技术整体规模较大，上海优势在于较强的产业带动能力，深圳优势则在于高度活跃的专利转移活动。

二、具体分析

（一）北京知识辐射带动效应突出

异地合作科技论文反映了地区知识创新与其他地区之间的联系，是表征知识溢出的重要指标。2013～2017 年，京沪深三地异地合作科技论文数量均呈波动增长态势，但是增幅较小，年均增速分别为 1.0%、1.3% 和 4.8%。从规模上看，北京优势极为明显，始终是上海的 3 倍以上、深圳的 11 倍以上，其知识创新的溢出效应突出。

（二）北京技术辐射总体规模强大

技术交易成交额是反映技术流动的重要指标，从流向上分为流向本地、流向外地和流向国外三部分，其中流向外地技术交易成交额是反映一个城市通过技术交易对国内其他地区辐射带动作用的重要指标。北京作为全国技术集散地，历年技术交易成交额占全国比重都在 1/3 左右，其中输出到国内其他省市的比重基本保持在一半以上。从输出到异地技术合同成交额看，北京 2017 年以超过 2000 亿元的规模居京沪深首位，分别是上海和深圳的 5.4 倍和 6.6 倍。

篇

图 7 - 2　京沪深异地合作科技论文数情况（2013~2017 年）

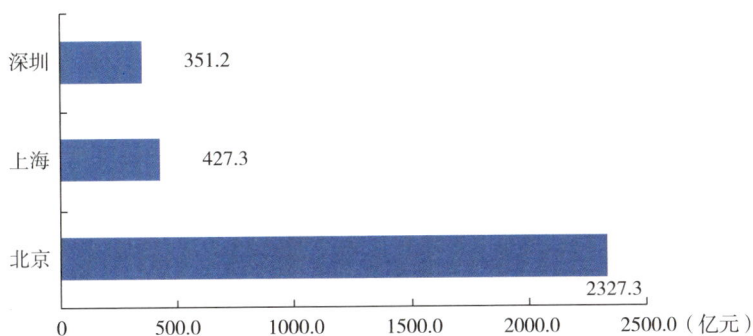

图 7 - 3　京沪深输出到异地技术合同成交额（2017 年）

（三）深圳专利技术溢出效果较强

异地专利转让数量反映地区技术创新与其他地区之间的联系，是表征技术流动的重要指标。2013~2017 年，京沪深三地异地专利转让数量均呈增长趋势，年均增速分别为 13.2%、17.7% 和 56.2%。从规模上看，2013~

2015 年北京始终相对领先，但优势不明显，2016 年和 2017 年深圳实现跨越式增长，尤其是 2017 年同比增长 1.2 倍，跃升至三地首位，分别是北京和上海的 1.9 倍和 1.8 倍。

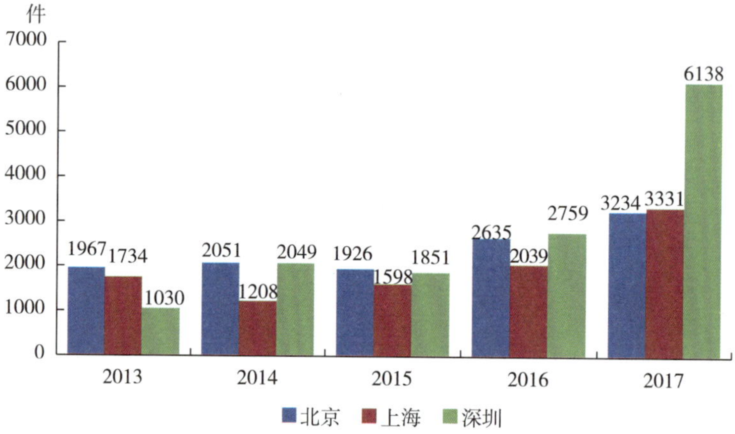

图 7－4　京沪深异地转让专利数情况（2013～2017 年）

从异地转让专利数占转让专利总数比重看，北京这一指标呈波动态势，整体上无明显增长，2017 年较 2013 年仅提升 0.6 个百分点。深圳的快速发展主要是从 2016 年出现快速上扬趋势，2016 年和 2017 年分别提高 9.4 个百分点和 12.7 个百分点。上海呈先降后升趋势，累计提升 3.1 个百分点。

（四）上海产业辐射带动作用明显

企业异地投资是区域产业对其他地区形成辐射带动作用的重要途径，投资高新技术企业情况能够反映通过产业资本带动其他区域科技创新的作用。上海企业异地投资高新技术企业占比整体呈平稳增长态势，始终保持在

50%以上，远高于深圳和北京。深圳这一指标逐年持续下降，5 年间降幅累计 14.8 个百分点，但始终高于北京。北京这一指标基本保持平稳，处于 30% ~40% 。

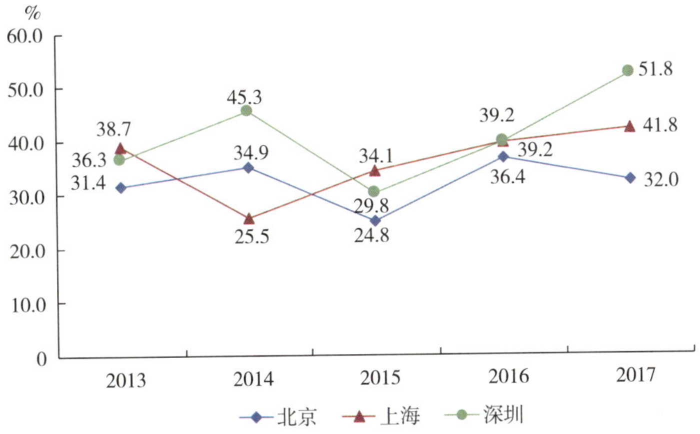

图 7 – 5 京沪深异地转让专利数占转让专利总数比重（2013 ~2017 年）

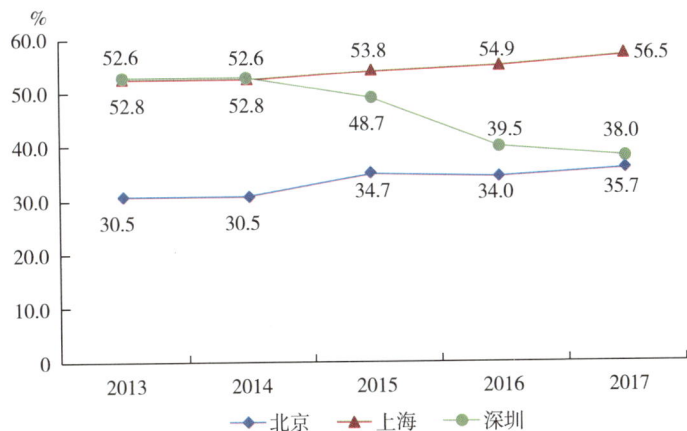

图 7 – 6 京沪深企业异地投资高新技术企业占比（2013 ~2017 年）

注：2013 年数据暂未获取，采用 2014 年数据代替。

三、小结

通过以上分析，在辐射功能方面，北京、上海和深圳都表现出稳定的增长趋势，又各自呈现出不同的特征。

北京作为全国的知识创新策源地，在知识溢出方面具有压倒性优势，这与高校院所云集的先天资源禀赋优势密切相关。规模宏大的技术市场也是北京发挥辐射功能的强大支撑，每年流向全国其他省市的技术合同份数和成交额分别在 3 万份和 1500 亿元以上。北京在专利转移和产业辐射上还具有较大的提升空间，尤其是专利转移，北京的专利拥有量在全国处于领先位置，大量的专利资源有待于挖掘。

上海优势在于较强的产业辐射能力，通过投资异地高新技术企业实现对其他区域科技创新的带动作用，企业异地投资高新技术企业占比始终保持在50%以上。上海的知识辐射不及北京，专利辐射不及深圳，在驱动自身发展的同时，应注意提升知识和技术的外溢效应。

深圳优势在于以专利为代表的知识产权转移活动的高度活跃，专利技术溢出效率较强，这与其企业主导创新的特征息息相关，知识辐射远低于京沪，知识溢出是其明显短板，这与前述集聚功能和原创功能评价中的结论一脉相承，深圳高校院所等知识创新主体缺乏，并且这种资源的集聚和发挥效应是很长时间积淀的结果，需要逐步积累并发挥作用。

第八章

主导功能评价

主导功能是一个地区把握关键性资源、掌握战略主动权程度的重要表现，是实现引领全球创新的方向。占据价值链和创新链的高端，以及提升在国际上的创新话语权和影响力的核心依托，是科技创新中心功能的终极体现。

一、总体情况

主导功能指标重点包括高研发投入企业、高技术产品、技术国际收入和知识产权四个方面。从评价结果看，深圳具有绝对优势，近 5 年主导功能均保持在京沪深首位，2017 年指数高达 261.6，分别是北京的 1.3 倍、上海的 2.0 倍。北京的主导功能优于上海，次于深圳，整体呈上升态势，2017 年达到 194.1，是 2013 年的近两倍。上海主导功能指数排名第三，且增长也相对缓慢，2017 年仅为 132.9。

从具体指标看，北京优势主要集中在高研发投入的企业数量多，上海优势主要集中在高技术产品和技术国际收入两方面，深圳优势主要集中在国际专利方面。

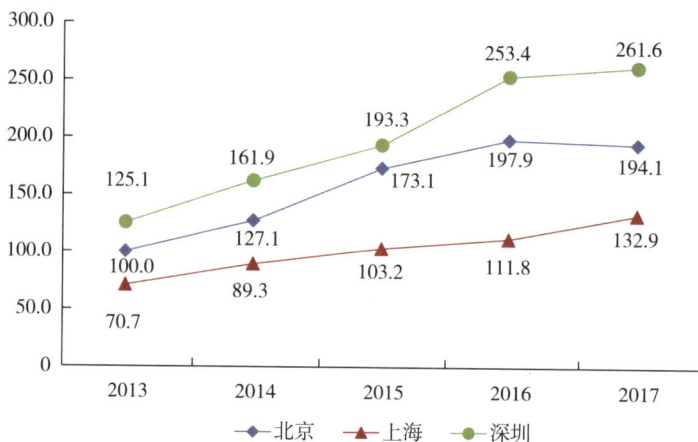

图 8 - 1 京沪深主导功能指数发展趋势（2013 ~ 2017 年）

二、具体分析

（一）北京高研发投入企业数量多

入围全球研发投入 2500 强企业数量反映了高研发投入的科技企业在全球的分布情况，长期以来，美国的高科技企业一直是全球创新的领头羊、推动者，但随着中国经济的不断发展，中国企业在研发投入上也不断加强，特别是京沪深三个科技创新中心的高研发投入企业数量不断攀升，在全球企业创新格局中逐渐形成强大势能。

从评价结果看，北京具有明显优势，2017 年 81 家企业入围，是深圳和上海的 2.0 倍，深圳和上海基本持平。从近 5 年变化来看，京沪深三地入围企业数量均保持了高速增长态势，其中北京 2013 年仅 18 家，2017 年迅速增长至 81 家，5 年累计增长了 3.5 倍。上海和深圳齐头并进，5 年分别累计增长了 3.4 倍和 4.1 倍。

值得注意的是，北京入围企业中大多是中石油、中国建筑集团、国铁集团、中车集团等大型央企，而深圳则以民营企业居多，特别是华为、中兴和腾讯 3 家企业 2017 年 R&D 经费合计为 1054.9 亿元，是北京地区全部企业 R&D 经费总量的 1.7 倍。

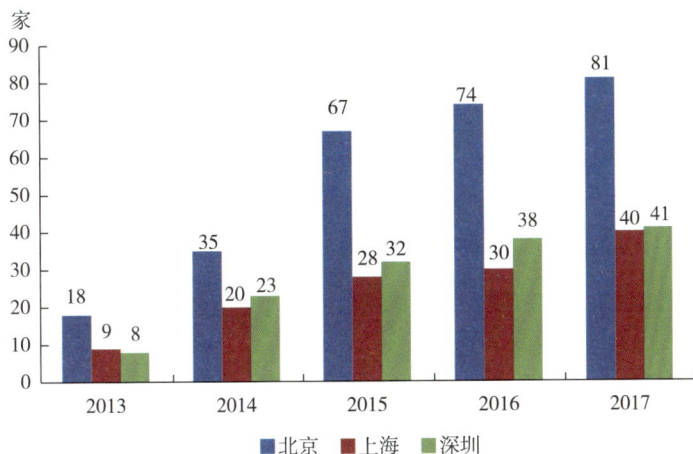

图 8-2 京沪深入围全球研发投入 2500 强企业数量发展趋势（2013~2017 年）

（二）上海商品出口结构持续优化

高技术产品出口额占商品出口额是反映高技术产品的国际竞争力和产品主导能力的指标。从高技术产品出口额总量来看，深圳具有绝对优势，2017

年高技术产品出口额达到 1145.7 亿美元，分别是北京的 10.1 倍、上海的 1.4 倍。从近 5 年变化来看，京沪深三地高技术产品出口全面萎缩，均处于下行态势。其中，深圳高技术产品出口额明显下滑，2017 年仅为 2013 年的 68.1%；2017 年，上海高技术产品出口额为 845.3 亿美元，是北京的 7.5 倍，近 5 年小幅下滑，2017 年为 2013 年的 95.3%；北京高技术产品出口额规模最小，且下滑速度最快，2017 年仅为 2013 年的 55.6%。

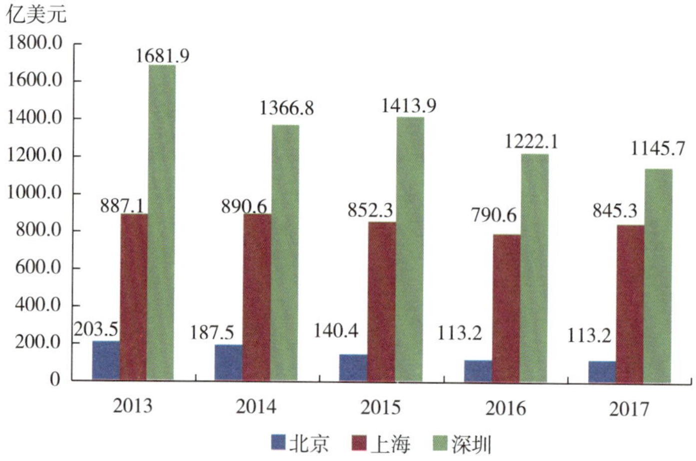

图 8-3 京沪深高技术产品出口额发展趋势（2013~2017 年）

从高技术产品出口额占商品出口额比重来看，上海具有优势，2017 年为 48.6%，分别高出北京和深圳 5.8 个百分点和 5.2 个百分点。深圳高技术产品出口额占商品出口额比重为 43.4%，居第二位，高于北京 0.6 个百分点。北京仅为 42.8%，居末位。从近 5 年变化来看，上海该指标处于缓慢增长态势，5 年累计增长 1.6 个百分点；深圳呈波动下降态势，5 年累计下降 8.2 个百分点；北京逐年快速下滑，5 年累计下降 18.5 个百分点。

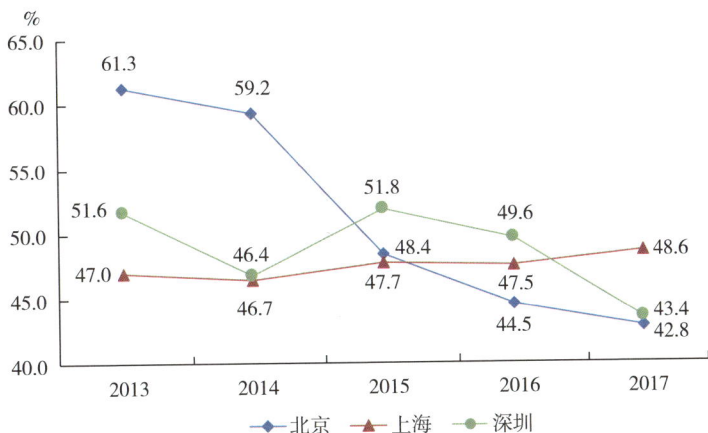

图 8 - 4　京沪深高技术产品出口额占商品出口额比重发展趋势 (2013 ~ 2017 年)

(三) 上海技术国际收入规模凸显

国际技术贸易是国际间技术资源优化配置与技术知识传播应用的重要手段，一国 (地区) 的技术国际收入状况反映了该国 (地区) 在国际上的科技实力和经济地位。

从技术国际收入看，上海具有显著优势，2017 年实现技术国际收入 156.2 亿美元，分别是北京的 1.8 倍，深圳的 2.6 倍。北京为 84.9 亿美元，是深圳的 1.4 倍。从近 5 年变化来看，上海逐年稳步提升，2017 年是 2013 年的 1.3 倍，年均增速为 5.9%；北京呈现明显下降趋势，2017 年仅为 2013 年的 86.6%；深圳先升后降，2013 ~ 2015 年逐年稳定增长，随后两年略有下滑。

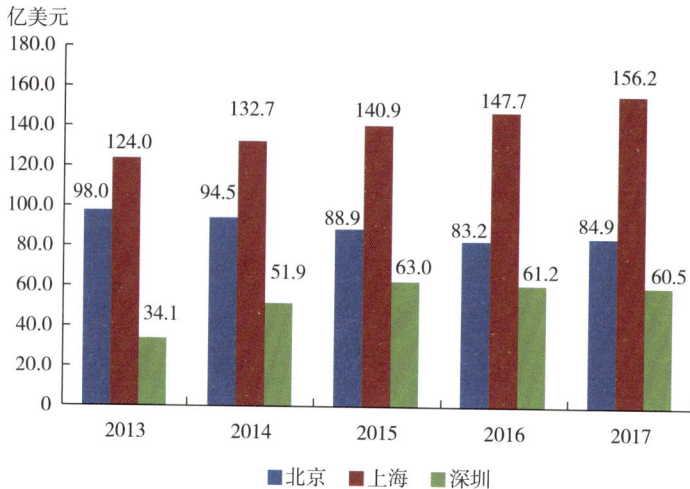

图 8－5 京沪深技术国际收入发展趋势（2013～2017 年）

（四）深圳知识产权主导能力突出

PCT 申请量是国际通用的反映一国或地区创新产出质量和技术国际竞争力的指标，可以反映知识产权主导能力和国际创新产出竞争力。

从评价结果看，深圳优势凸显，2017 年 PCT 申请量高达 20457 件，分别是北京的 4.0 倍、上海的 9.7 倍，仅华为一家企业的 PCT 申请量就达到 4024 件，接近北京申请总量的 80%，是上海的 1.9 倍。与上海相比，北京 PCT 申请量具有优势，2017 年为 5069 件，是上海的 2.4 倍。从近 5 年变化看，京沪深三地均呈现快速增长态势。其中，深圳增长迅猛，5 年实现翻番，年均增速为 19.4%；北京也呈现增长趋势，2017 年是 2013 年的 1.7 倍，年均增速为 14.2%；上海增长最快，2017 年是 2013 年的 2.4 倍，年均增速为 24.1%。

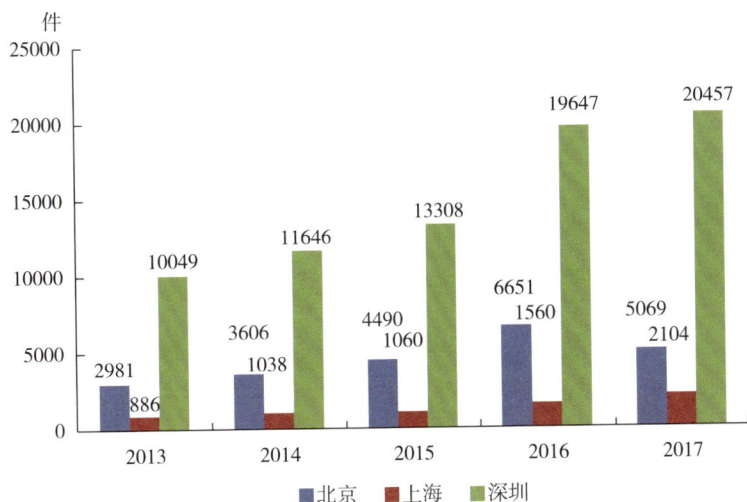

图 8 – 6　京沪深 PCT 申请量发展趋势（2013～2017 年）

三、小结

通过以上分析，在主导功能方面，北京、上海和深圳都呈现持续增长态势，在主导因素方面各具特点。

北京主导功能的优势在于高研发投入企业数量较多，在入围全球研发投入 2500 强企业数量方面远高于上海和深圳，但这些企业以央企为主。北京在高技术产品出口、技术国际收入方面呈下降趋势，国际专利布局仍需加强。

上海主导功能优势主要表现在高技术产品出口和技术国际收入两方面，

2017 年高技术产品出口额占商品出口额比重领先北京和深圳，实现技术国际收入远高于北京和深圳，外向型经济质量不断提升。在高研发投入企业和国际专利布局两方面还有较大的提升空间。

深圳国际专利方面的优势非常明显，PCT 专利申请数量远高于北京和上海，以华为为代表的领军型科技企业表现尤为突出。深圳高研发投入企业的整体数量、商品出口结构和技术国际收入三个方面仍需努力。

指标解释

（1）**万名从业人员 R&D 人员数**。R&D 人员是创新最为重要的人力资源之一。R&D 人员是指参与研究与试验发展项目研究、管理和辅助工作的人员，包括项目（课题）组人员、科技行政管理人员和直接为项目（课题）活动提供服务的辅助人员，是反映科技创新人力资源水平的主要指标。万名从业人员 R&D 人员数是反映相对就业规模创新人力资源状况的指标。

（2）**R&D 经费投入强度**。即 R&D 经费支出与 GDP 比值，是国际上通用的衡量科技财力投入强度最为重要、最为综合的指标。发达国家在人均 GDP 达到 3000~4000 美元时这一比例所达到的最低水平为 2.5%。

（3）**高端仪器设备数量**。高端仪器设备指原值在 500 万元（含 500 万元）以上，纳入法人单位资产管理的单台（套）科研仪器设备。高端仪器设备是科学研究和技术创新的基础条件，其应用水平是衡量一个国家（地区）科技发展水平和潜力的重要标志。

（4）**科研机构和高校数量**。科研机构是指从事科学研究活动的机构，即以基础科学研究和应用科学研究为主业的机构。高校指普通高等学校，是由国家教育部或省级教育行政部门（含自治区、直辖市等）主管的实行高等教育的学校。科研机构和高校是我国创新体系的重要组成部分，承担着科学研究的重任，其数量能够反映区域智力资源的聚集程度。

（5）**入选全球高被引科学家数量**。全球"高被引科学家"名单是由科睿唯安采用最新数据和先进算法，通过对 21 个大学科技领域近十年被 SCI 收录的自然和社会科学领域论文进行分析评估，并将所属领域同一年度他引频次在前 1% 的论文进行排名统计后得出的。入选"高被引科学家"名单，意味着该学者在其所研究领域具有世界级影响力，其科研成果为该领域发展做出了较大贡献。

（6）**基础研究经费占全社会研发经费比重**。R&D 按照活动类型分为基础研究、应用研究和试验发展，其中基础研究是指为了获得关于现象和可观察事实的基本原理的新知识（提示客观事物的本质、运动规律，获得新发现、新学科）而进行的实验性或理论性工作，它不以任何专门或特定的应用或使用为目的。基础研究经费占全社会研发经费比重是国际通用的反映原始创新能力的指标。

（7）**SCI 论文数量**。国际上通常用 SCI（科学引文索引）数据库评价基础研究成果，它收录了经过遴选的世界各国重要科技期刊上发表的论文，也就是大家常说的"SCI 论文"。

（8）**万人发明专利拥有量**。专利的数量是反映一个国家（地区）科技活动产出的重要指标，发明专利数量又是其中更为重要的指标。发明专利拥有量反映在某一时点上有效发明专利的存量。

（9）**高端产业就业人员占全社会就业人员比重**。高端产业包括知识密集型服务业和高技术制造业，分别反映了第二产业和第三产业的中高端产业情况。高端产业频繁地使用高新技术，是吸纳高素质劳动力就业的主要行业。高端产业就业人员占全社会就业人员比重反映了全社会从业人员中高技能、高素质人才的比重，同时能够反映产业结构优化升级情况。

（10）**新产品销售收入**。产品创新活动是企业最主要的创新活动，新产品产出是将企业创新活动转化为现实生产力的重要标志。

（11）**劳动生产率**。劳动生产率是指劳动者在一定时期内创造的劳动成果与其相适应的劳动消耗量的比值。劳动生产率是从劳动节约的角度反映经济发展方式转变的指标，为生产总值与就业人员数之比。

（12）资本生产率。资本生产率是指一定时期内单位资本创造的产出，该指标衡量了单位资本的产出能力，单位资本产出越高，资本生产率就越高。资本生产率反映的是资本投入与经济产出之间的关系，即生产总值与资本投入之比。

（13）异地合作科技论文数。异地合作科技论文数反映某一地区知识创新与其他地区之间的联系，是表征知识溢出的重要指标。

（14）输出到异地技术合同成交额。技术交易成交额是反映技术流动的重要指标，从流向上分为流向本地、流向外地和流向国外三部分，其中流向异地技术交易成交额是反映一个地区通过技术转移对国内其他地区辐射带动作用的重要指标。

（15）异地转让专利数占转让专利总数比重。异地专利转让数量反映某一地区技术创新与其他地区之间的联系，是表征技术流动的重要指标。异地转让专利数占转让专利总数比重反映技术跨区域流动的程度。

（16）企业异地投资高新技术企业占比。指本区域企业投资的高新技术企业中，注册地在外地的高新技术企业所占的比例。该指标能够反映通过产业资本带动其他区域科技创新的作用。

（17）入围全球研发投入 2500 强企业数量。欧盟委员会科学与知识服务机构联合研究中心每年发布世界企业研发投入 2500 强企业名单，包含了全球研发资金投入最多的 2500 家企业。入围榜单企业数量能够反映一国或地区企业在全球的研发地位。

（18）高技术产品出口额占商品出口额比重。高技术产品出口额是根据海关总署《高技术产品目录》从商品出口额中分离出的数据，按原产地进行统计。高技术产品出口额占商品出口额比重可以反映高技术产品的国际竞争力。

（19）**技术国际收入**。国际技术贸易是国际间技术资源优化配置与技术知识传播应用的重要手段，技术国际收入主要指的是通过向他国转让专利、非专利发明、商标等知识产权、提供 R&D 服务和其他技术服务而获得的收入。一国（地区）的技术国际收入状况反映着该国（地区）在国际上的科技实力和经济地位。

（20）**PCT 专利申请数**。PCT 国际申请量是全球公认的用来衡量一个国家、地区以及企业的创新能力，尤其是国际竞争力的重要指标，是评估知识产权与专利竞争力的首要度量衡。重视 PCT 国际专利申请，对于在竞争中完善专利布局、获取更多市场、赢得更大经济效益至关重要。

参考文献

［1］JAFFE A B，TRAJTENBERG M，HENDERSON R. Geographic Locali-zation of Knowledge Spillovers as Evidenced by Patent Citations ［J］. The Quar-terly Journal of Economics，1993，108（3）：577－598.

［2］EC. European Innovation Scoreboard 2017 ［R］. European Commis-sion，2017.

［3］OECD. Managing National Innovation Systems ［R］. Paris：OECD，1999.

［4］玄兆辉，朱迎春，刘辉峰，等. 国家创新指数报告 2016－2017 ［R］. 北京：科学技术文献出版社，2017.

［5］柳卸林，等. 中国区域创新能力评价报告 2017 ［R］. 北京：科学技术文献出版社，2017.

［6］2thinknow. Innovation Cities? Index 2016－2017：Global ［EB/OL］. 2017－02－22. http：//www. innovation－cities. com/innovation－cities－index－2016－2017－global/9774.

［7］杜德斌，何舜辉. 全球科技创新中心的内涵、功能与组织结构 ［J］. 中国科技论坛，2016（2）：10－15.

［8］廖明中，胡彧彬. 国际科技创新中心的演进特征及启示 ［J］. 城市观察，2019（3）：117－126.

［9］黄静静，张志娟，李富强. 全球科技创新中心评价分析及对北京市建设启示 ［J］. 全球科技经济瞭望，2018，33（6）：56－63＋70.

［10］张士运，王健，庞立艳，等. 科技创新中心的功能与评价研究 ［J］. 世界科技研究与发展，2018，40（2）：61－70.

Functional Evaluation Study Group of Beijing – Shanghai – Shenzhen Center of Science and Technology Innovation

Group Leader：Zhang Shiyun

Members of the Group：

Wang Jian   Pang Liyan   Yao Changle   Wang Lifang

Li Dongmei   Lu Xin   Zhao Dandan   Li Jingyu

Consultant：

Wang Jun   Survey Office of the National Bureau of Statistics
            in Beijing   Deputy Chairman

Shi Linfen   Huazhong University of Science and Technology
                                                Professor

Xuan Zhaohui   Chinese Academy of Science and Technology
              for Development   Researcher

Li Shizhu   Beijing Education Examination Authority   Dean

He Ping   China Statistical Research of National Bureau of
           Statistics   Researcher

Song Weiguo   China Society for Science and Technology Indi-
             cators   Secretary – General

Preface

As an important part of building an innovative country, the Center of Science and Technology Innovation is the core support for the construction of a strong science and technology power. On February 26, 2014, when General Secretary Xi Jinping inspected in Beijing, he clearly mentioned that Beijing should develop to help the construction of a national science and technology innovation center for the first time. In May 2014, General Secretary Xi Jinping proposed that Shanghai should accelerate its entry into the globally influential science and technology innovation center during his inspection in Shanghai. On July 1, 2017, General Secretary Xi Jinping personally witnessed the National Development and Reform Commission and the governments of Guangdong, Hong Kong and Macao jointly signed the "Framework Agreement for Deepening the Cooperation between Guangdong, Hong Kong and Macao to

Promote the Construction of the Guangdong – Hong Kong – Macao Greater Bay Area", which clearly defined the positioning of the international center of science technology innovation in the Guangdong – Hong Kong – Macao Greater Bay Area. Moreover, Shenzhen, as one of the core cities of Guangdong – Hong Kong – Macao Greater Bay Area, shoulders the heavy responsibility of leading the construction of this center.

In order to scientifically measure and evaluate the process of establishing the Beijing – Shanghai – Shenzhen Center of Science and Technology Innovation, the research is based on the in – depth study of the connotation and function of the science and technology innovation center, with the five functions of "agglomeration, innovation, drive, radiation, and dominance" as the framework, using the domestic and international authoritative indicator system as a reference. Based on the data reliability, comparability and continuity, the index system builds five first – level indicators and 20 second – level indicators to form a function evaluation index system for science and technology innovation centers. In addition, the report conducts an empirical comparative study from the horizontal and vertical dimensions and analyzes their respective strengths and weaknesses and the development trend of the past five years. Besides, it systematically reflects the main functional characteristics and status of the construction of the Beijing, Shanghai and Shenzhen science and technology innovation centers. This report is a quantitative and comprehensive evaluation report of the functions of the Beijing – Shanghai – Shenzhen Center of Science and Technology Innovation.

During the preparation of the report, we received warm help and careful guidance from the experts and scholars of the Chinese Academy of Science and Technology for Development, China Society for Science and Technology Indicators, China Statistical Research of National Bureau of Statistics, the Huazhong University of Science and Technology and other think tanks. The function evaluation of the Science and Technology Innovation Center is still in the exploratory stage. Thus, the content and results of the evaluation report only represent the views of the research group. If there is any inadequacy, please feel free to raise criticisms and suggestions from all walks of life to help us continuously improve. We sincerely hope that this study will provide a window for the society to understand the status of the Beijing – Shanghai – Shenzhen Center of Science and Technology Innovation.

Content

Chapter I

Theoretical Background

1. Connotation of Science and Innovation Center

Combining relevant research both at home and abroad, as well as the practical experience of other world – renowned innovation centers, we believe that we should deeply explore and understand the connotation of science and technology innovation centers from three aspects: Endowment, function and meaning. Science and technology innovation center is a center of the agglomeration of high – end innovation resources and rich cultural atmosphere, which has outstanding original innovation capability, significant innovation – driven effect and strong radiation ability. It is the source of new ideas, knowledge, technologies, products, formats that dominate the technological innovation system. It can be leader of scientific and technological innovation in the country and even the world. Meanwhile, it is the core support for participation in global innovation competition.

Therefore, the Science and Technology Innovation Center should have world – leading knowledge and technological achievements, outstanding scientists and entrepreneurs, internationally influential universities and research institutions and innovative enterprises with international competitiveness. It should have a social environment suitable for innovation and entrepreneurship, a mature capital market and advanced institutional arrangements to represent the world's most advanced productive forces, realize the open integration of the innovation chain and the industrial chain and lead the scientific and technological progress and economic development. The center is different from a simple science center or the technology R&D center in its rich connotations, extensions and development laws.

2. Functions of Science and Innovation Center

Combined with relevant research at home and abroad, the development of science and technology innovation centers should have the following signs: First, it can gather various innovative elements and influential scientific research organizations to attract high – quality talents and have developed capital markets. Second, it has relatively complete and appropriate innovation chain and industry chain, which can quickly realize industrialization on the spot while forming internationally influential scientific and technological achievements and ideas. Third, there are a large number of innovative enterprises with high growth, vitality and international influence, occupying a leading position in the industry. Fourth, there is a living – friendly and business – friendly environment and a culture that tolerates failure and is multi – inclusive. Focusing on the perspective of innovation chain and innovation ecology, and analyzing from the perspective of knowledge production, application and diffusion, we believe that the science and technology innovation center should have the following five functions:

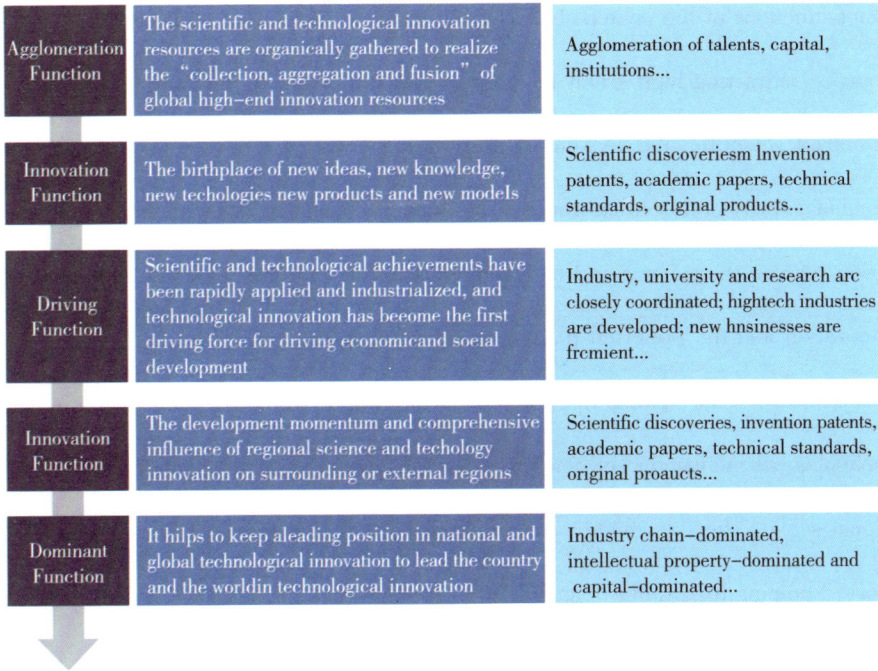

Agglomeration Function	The scientific and technological innovation resources are organically gathered to realize the "collection, aggregation and fusion" of global high-end innovation resources	Agglomeration of talents, capital, institutions...
Innovation Function	The birthplace of new ideas, new knowledge, new techologies new products and new models	Sclentific discoveriesm lnvention patents, academic papers, technical standards, orlginal products...
Driving Function	Scientific and technological achievements have been rapidly applied and industrialized, and technological innovation has beeome the first driving force for driving economicand soeial development	Industry, university and research arc closely coordinated; hightech industries are developed; new hnsinesses are frcmient...
Innovation Function	The development momentum and comprehensive influence of regional science and techology innovation on surrounding or external regions	Scientific discoveries, invention patents, academic papers, technical standards, original proaucts...
Dominant Function	It hilps to keep aleading position in national and global technological innovation to lead the country and the worldin technological innovation	Industry chain-dominated, intellectual property-dominated and capital-dominated...

Figure 1 – 1   Five Core Functions of the Science and Technology Innovation Center

(1) Agglomeration Function

The agglomeration function gathers scientific and technological innovation resources, including talents, capital, R&D and service organizations and enterprises. It is the foundation of the science and technology innovation center, which reflects the innovation investment as well as the cultivation and flow of innovation elements and provides support for industrial upgrading and economic transformation and development. The agglomeration function is the key to a good innovation eco-system. A powerful agglomeration function provides a solid foundation for innovation and entrepreneurship in the region and is a prerequisite for the realization of other functions of the center. Only by relying on unique science and education resources, attracting high – end talent resources from around the world, possessing abundant scientific and technological resources, having convenient and efficient technology service resources and a large number of innovative technology enterprise resources can the science and technology center become the leader of technological innovation and the preferred place for innovation and entrepreneurship.

However, the spatial distribution of innovative resources and scientific and technological innovation activities are extremely uneven at the global scale or regional scale. They are highly concentrated in a few regions or cities around the world, bulging highly like "nails". These resources become the core support for the development and the comprehensive strength of science and technology in the country.

To sum up, the embodiment of the agglomeration function includes the accumulation of people, finances, materials and institutions, etc.

(2) Innovation Function

Innovation function is related to the expression of knowledge production. As a result of gathering a group of innovative talents and first – class universities, scientific research institutions and innovative enterprises, it will inevitably form a combination of talent cultivation, knowledge innovation and technological innovation.

It can result in a series of innovation achievements and become the birthplace of new ideas, knowledge, technologies, products and models.

The innovation function is the overall ability of a regional science and technology innovation, which includes scientific exploration and discovery as well as theoretical formation of technology and major inventions. The primary performance of innovation function depends on the ability and level of theoretical basic research and applied basic research. It doesn't only mark the strength of the innovation ability of a country and region, but also the fundamental driving force for the sustainable development of international metropolises. American scholar V. Bush once pointed out: "A country that relies on other countries in new basic scientific knowledge will have a slow industrial progress. No matter how sophisticated its mechanical skills are, its competitive position in world trade will be weak."

Forms of presentation: Basic research funding, publication and citation of high – level papers, invention and application of patents, etc.

(3) Driving Function

The driving function is the performance of knowledge application. In the current world, the conversion cycle of scientific and technological achievements is becoming shorter and shorter. Innovations are changing and the popularization and application of innovations are accelerating, presenting a situation where the slow fish can be easily caught and eaten by the fast fish. If the innovation results cannot be transformed quickly into real productivity, the value cannot be realized. To this end, the core to promote the development of technology and economy of our society is to enables every part of the innovation ecology to commercialize their innovation achievements and protect respective interests, thus technological achievements can be realized to motivate industry revolution through product innovation, market innovation and management innovation.

There is a common problem in the world's scientific and technological industry that how to make scientific and technological achievements enter the enterprise from the laboratory and turn into the products that the society needs. This process is called "the Nightmare Era" by scientists in the United States and Europe, and the "Valley of Death" by Japanese scientists because many scientific research results only live in laboratories and academic journals.

In a nutshell, the driving function refers to the ability of transforming scientific and technological achievements into real productivity. It includes two connotations: The first refers to the commercialization and industrialization of scientific and technological achievements with use value produced during scientific research and technological development; The second is that new knowledge, thinking, concept, designs and ideas are closely integrated with science and technology into real productivity. The driving function can also be understood from three levels: At the micro level, we should pay attention to the transformation of technology achievements and product development; At the meso level, we should focus on the integration of science and technology resources, open sharing and the combination of production, study and research to achieve results transformation; At the macro level, we are determined to reform and innovate by relying on scientific and technological progress, nurturing emerging industries and promoting structural adjustment and transforming development methods.

Its main form is to have a relatively complete and appropriate innovation chain and industrial chain and can quickly realize industrialization on the spot while forming internationally influential scientific and technological achievements and ideas. The basic implementation methods include economic output, high – tech industrial structure, production efficiency, etc.

(4) Radiation Function

The radiation function is a manifestation of knowledge diffusion. The Innovation Center has more innovation achievements, new knowledge, new technologies and global influential enterprises. Therefore, it has a comparative advantage around the world. It will inevitably give powerful innovation radiation function to the whole country and even the world.

Radiation in science and technology innovation refers to the driving force and comprehensive influence of regional science and technology innovation on the development of surrounding or external regions, including the flow and transfer of patents, talents, technology, market and other elements as well as the dissemination of scientific and technological innovations. These are the basic forms of motion that maintain contact and interaction among regions, measured primarily through both sources and flows. Radiation sources refer to areas with relatively high levels of technological innovation. The medium of radiation is mainly reflected in traffic conditions, information dissemination, personnel mobility, capital flow and technology transfer. Radiation flow refers to the ability of connecting between radiation sources and foreign technology.

A science and technology innovation center is responsible for the high – end radiation through scientific and technological achievements and innovation elements. Besides, it shoulders the mission of technological innovation and industrial upgrading. Its spillover radiates from surrounding areas to other external regions, cities and provinces through technologies, capital, talents, information, management, policies, etc. Moreover, it drives the fine management of the cities and the construction of ecological civilization through the transfer of green technology. In addition, it plays a leading role in the country and the world through creating innovative ideas, institutional mechanisms, innovative environments and cultural environments that have a nationwide promotional value. Therefore, it can truly be an example of a science and technology innovation center, high – end industrial source and ecological construction demonstration city. The radiation function is the key to the center as role model in the country and the world. This function can be characterized from the dimensions of knowledge technology spillover, talent flow and cooperation and communication.

Knowledge technology spillover is one of the important concepts of agglomeration, innovation and regional growth. From the perspective of the cultivation of core competitiveness, Krugman believes that knowledge technology spillover is the result of knowledge application, the economic effect and form of knowledge management. Some scholars think that the existence and measurability of knowledge technology spillovers can be studied from different dimensions such as patent citation, innovation output and spatial distribution of innovation activities. It becomes an important factor affecting spatial agglomeration, innovation and regional growth. Factors such as talent mobility, R&D cooperation, entrepreneurs' entrepreneurship and trade investment are important mechanisms for knowledge and technology spillovers.

The main forms of radiation function include knowledge spillover, technology flow, and industrial driving ability.

(5) Dominant Function

The dominant function is the comprehensive performance of knowledge production, application and diffusion. In the innovation ecosystem, a world – class innovative enterprise and first – class innovation achievements are formed, occupying the high end of the value chain and innovation chain, which will inevitably have a profound impact on global technological innovation and industrial development, thus eventually forming a dominant pattern and becoming the core of the national innovation strategy. This function is considered as the ultimate performance of the innovation center. Only with the science and technology innovation center can we have the ability to coordinate and innovate resources and lead the direction of innovation.

The dominant function is to measure the key innovation resources, master the initiative and control of a region. A science and technology innovation center must have this function to master the overall situation. But this kind of dominance is not an administrative intervention but precisely a market behavior and plays a decisive role in resource allocation.

Main form of this function is it equips with a large number of innovative enterprises with high growth, vitality and international influence, leading in several industrial fields; firmly grasp key nodes, key elements, initiative decision – making power and resources allocation power etc. Through intellectual property, capital and industrial chain so as to obtain unique benefits in the industry chain and value chain.

Chapter II

Indicator Construction

The functional evaluation of the science and technology innovation center is a systematic work requiring a solid theoretical background, a reasonable framework, a scientific evaluation method and reliable basic data. Based on the five functional theories of the science and technology innovation center, this report builds the functional evaluation index system with reference to the authoritative scientific and technological innovation evaluation index system both at home and abroad.

1.　Construction Idea

Firstly, it uses the "Five Major Functions" theory of the science and technology innovation center as a framework. The functional evaluation index system of the science and technology innovation center is constructed with the theoretical framework of "agglomeration function, original function, driving function, radiation function and dominant function", combined with the connotation and function of the center. Among them, the agglomeration function is characterized from four aspects of innovation: Talent, finance, material and institution. The innovation function is expressed in both innovation input and innovation output. The driving function performs through industrial optimization and efficiency improvement. The radiation function includes knowledge, technology and industry. The dominant function is characterized by technology leadership and industry leadership.

Secondly, **it uses the domestic and international authoritative indicator systems as references**. It fully draw on the internationally renowned innovation evaluation index such as the Silicon Valley Index, the European Innovation Scoreboard and the Global Innovation Index, as well as the design thinkings, index selection and evaluation methods of the domestic authoritative innovation evaluation system such as the China Innovation Index and China's regional innovation capability evaluation.

Thirdly, **it uses national strategic goals and international benchmarking as a direction**. One – third of the indicators designed in the indicator system comes from the scientific and technological development goals described in the documents such as the "the 13th Five – year Plan for the Country's Scientific and Technological Progress" and "National Program for Long – and Medium – Term term Development", highlighting the strategic positioning of the science and technology innovation center. In the designing of specific indicators, we focus on the use of internationally accepted indicators, such as the proportion of R&D expenditures in the whole society as a percentage of regional GDP and labor productivity.

Fourthly, **it is based on data reliability**, **stability and continuity**. To guarantee that the calculation results are true and reliable, the data of the science and technology innovation center's function index calculation is based on authoritative institutions, including the China Statistical Yearbook on Science and Technology, China Statistical Yearbook and other public information, Institute of Scientific and Technical Information of China and other departments and international author-

ity list, etc.

2. Indicator System

(1) Selection Principle

Whether the evaluation results are objective and accurate depends on the in-

formation contained in each evaluation index. Therefore, the selection of indicators

to evaluate the function of science and technology innovation center is the core of

the establishment of the evaluation system. Besides, it is also the key to defining

whether the evaluation system is scientific, objective and feasible. The following

principles are important for selecting evaluation indicators:

Scientific Principle: The construction of the index system should be based on

objectiveness and reasonable theory. At the same time, scientific methods should

be used in the processing of data and index measurement to ensure the authenticity

of the evaluation results.

Systematic Principle: There should be a certain logic between indicators. It

can reflect the status of the construction of science and technology innovation cen-

ters from different aspects and can reflect the internal relationship between the

"five functions" and form an organic unity more accurately. The construction of the indicator system should be hierarchical in forming an inseparable evaluation system layer by layer from top to bottom and from macro to micro level.

Principle of Comprehensive Balance: The indicator system can cover all aspects of the science and technology innovation center, comprehensively considering the relationship among various elements. Lower levels of indicators should be able to fully reflect the indicators of the upper level. Meanwhile, attention should be paid to the levels of indicators, the number of indicators, and the balance between the absolute and relative indicators.

Principle of Comparability: Each indicator in the indicator system must reflect the common attributes of the evaluated objects and the common content of the attributes of the evaluated objects under the same measurement range, measurement caliber and measurement method.

Principle of Operability: Not only the selected evaluation indicators should be representative, but the indicator data should be easy to collect. Besides, the information should be reliable and easy to compare and evaluate in time and space.

（2）Construction Method

By referring to the evaluation indicators adopted by the domestic and foreign innovation evaluation system, combined with the research on the agglomeration function, original function, driving function, radiation function and the dominant function connotation, the function evaluation of the science and technology innovation center adopts the tree evaluation index system and uses the analytic hierarchy process. The indicators are determined layer by layer from top to bottom, and finally form a secondary indicator system, including 5 first – level indicators and 20 second – level indicators. See Table 2 – 1 for details.

Table 2 – 1   The Function Evaluation Indicator System of
the Science Technology Innovation Center

	First – level Indicators	Second – level Indicators
Functional Comprehensive Index of Science and Technology Innovation Center	Agglomeration Function	the number of R&D (Research and Development) personnel of 10000 employees
		R&D investment intensity
		the number of high – end instruments and equipment
		the number of research institutions and universities
	Innovation Function	the number of highly cited scientists in the world
		the proportion of basic research funding to R&D expenditure in the whole society
		the number of SCI papers
		patent ownership of 10000 people
	Driving Function	the proportion of employed people in high – end industries to employed people in the whole society
		new product sales revenue
		labor productivity
		capital productivity
	Radiation Function	the number of co – authored scientific papers in different places
		output to off – site technology contract turnover
		the proportion of the number of patents transferred from different places to the total number of transferred patents
		the proportion of high – tech enterprises in different places invested by local enterprises
	Dominant Function	the number of top 2500 companies in the global R&D investment
		the proportion of the export value of high – tech products to merchandise exports
		international revenue of technology
		the number of PCT patent applications

The five first – level indicators fully reflect the core functions of the science and technology innovation center. The 20 secondary indicators support the five functions of the science and technology innovation center from the perspective of the input – output – performance chain.

1) Agglomeration Function Indicator

The agglomeration function gathers scientific and technological innovation resources and it is the foundation of the science and technology innovation center. This function is represented by four aspects: Talent, finance, materials and institutions. The specific indicators are the number of R&D (Research and Development) personnel of 10000 employees, R&D investment intensity, the number of high – end instruments and equipment and the number of scientific research institutions and universities.

2) Innovation Function Indicator

The innovation function is the overall ability of a region's innovation in science and technology, including both the input and the output capacity of innovation. Therefore, relevant indicators are set from two dimensions of input and output. The investment includes both talents and funds. The indicators are the number of highly cited scientists in the world, and the proportion of basic research funding to R&D expenditure in the whole society. The output is reflected in both knowledge and technology with specific indicators of the number of SCI papers and patent ownership of 10000 people.

3) Driving Function Indicator

The driving function refers to the transformation of scientific and technological achievements into real productivity, which has a positive impact on regional economic and social development, thus achieving the goal of innovation – driven development including optimization of industrial structure and improvement of production efficiency. The specific indicators include the proportion of employed people in high – end industries to employed people in the whole society, new product sales revenue, labor productivity and capital productivity. Among them, high – end industries refer to knowledge – intensive service industries and high – tech manufacturing industries, which reflect the improvement of industrial structure from both manufacturing and service industries.

4) Radiation Function Indicator

The radiation function refers to the driving force and comprehensive influence of regional science and technology innovation on the development of surrounding areas or external areas, mainly in the aspects of knowledge spillovers, technology flows and industry driving capacity. The specific indicators include the number of co – authored scientific papers in different places and output to off – site technology contract turnover, the proportion of the number of patents transferred from different places to the total number of transferred patents, and the proportion of high – tech enterprises in different places invested by local enterprises.

5) Dominant Function Indicator

The dominant function is the ultimate performance of the science and technology innovation center. Only by giving full play to the dominant functions of the science and technology innovation center can we have the ability to coordinate and innovate resources and even lead innovation development. It is performed from two aspects in the indicator system: Industry – led and technology – led. The specific indicators include the number of top 2500 companies in the global R&D investment, the proportion of high – tech products exports to merchandise exports, international revenue of technology, and the number of PCT patent applications.

3. Evaluation Method

(1) Comprehensive Evaluation Method

To obtain a comprehensive index, the multi – index comprehensive evaluation method combines the information of multiple indicators describing different aspects of the evaluation objects, thereby making an overall evaluation of the object with horizontal or vertical comparison. The basic idea to reflect the overall picture of the evaluation object. To achieve it, organizing a plurality of individual indicators to form a comprehensive indicator including various aspects is of great necessity. From a mathematical point of view, it is a problem of classifying or sorting the operating conditions of n evaluation objects when the m – item evaluation indexes $x1$, $x2$, $x3$, $\cdots$, xm are selected.

The function evaluation of the science and technology innovation center adopts a linear comprehensive evaluation model:

$$y_i = \sum_{j=0}^{m} w_j x_{ij}$$

Where x_{ij} is the j – th index value of the i – th evaluation object, w_j is the weight coefficient of the evaluation index x_{ij} ($w_j \geqslant 0$, $\sum w_j = 1$) , and y_i is the i – th ($i = 1, 2, \cdots, n$) comprehensive evaluation value of the evaluated objects.

(2) Indicator Weight Setting

It can be seen from the formula of the linear comprehensive evaluation model that weight is one of the important factors affecting the comprehensive evaluation results. In the comprehensive weighted evaluation of multiple indicators, the determination of the weight of each indicator is very critical, which is directly related to the conclusion of the analysis.

Through the research on the authoritative innovation evaluation system at home and abroad, it is found that the European Innovation Scoreboard, the Global Innovation Index and the China Innovation Index all use the equal weight method to empower the indicators. The importance of drawing on the weighting method of international authoritative evaluation system, and taking into account that the agglomeration function, original function, driving function, radiation function and dominant function are equally important to the establishment of science and technology innovation centers. The lack or weakening of any part will lead to the "cask effect" . Therefore, the index empowerment uses the equal weight method.

(3) Nondimensionalization of Indicators

In the multi – index evaluation system, due to the different natures of each evaluation index, it usually has different dimensions and orders of magnitude. When the levels between the indicators differ greatly and the analysis is performed directly with the original index values, the role of the higher – value indicators in the comprehensive analysis will be highlighted while the effect of the lower – level indicators will be relatively weakened. Therefore, in order to ensure the reliability of the results, the original indicator data needs to be standardized.

Beijing, Shanghai and Shenzhen have clearly established the science and technology innovation center. Therefore, these three places are selected for empirical evaluation. The combination of horizontal and vertical evaluation methods is adopted. Considering that the construction of science and technology innovation center is a gradual process, the index calculation and evaluation use the fixed ratio method to carry out the dimensionless treatment of the basic indicators in the empirical evaluation.

Chapter III

Overall Evaluation

The construction of science and technology innovation centers in Beijing, Shanghai and Shenzhen has made remarkable progress, especially with the support of the central and local governments. From the results of the function evaluation of the science and technology innovation center, the comprehensive index of functions the Beijing – Shanghai – Shenzhen Center of Science and Technology Innovation continue to grow. The five first – level indicator of agglomeration function, innovation function, driving function, radiation function and dominant function also shows different growth trends and gets further strengthened.

1. Comprehensive Index of Functions Has a Stable Growth Momentum

From 2013 to 2017, the total comprehensive index of functions of the Beijing – Shanghai – Shenzhen Center of Science and Technology Innovation showed an overall growth trend. In 2017, it reached 146.5, 104.0 and 128.0 respectively. Beijing ranked first, and Shenzhen and Shanghai ranked second and third respectively.

The gap among the three places showed an expanding trend during the period and then showed the parallel development from 2013 to 2015. The gap remained stable in the past two years. From 2013 to 2017, the Beijing – Shanghai – Shenzhen Center of Science and Technology Innovation's comprehensive index of functions increased by 46.5, 27.9 and 43.8 respectively. An obvious growth in Shanghai can be noticed in 2017. The data increased by 9.2 compared with the previous year, which is significantly higher than Shenzhen and Beijing's 8.5 and 8.3.

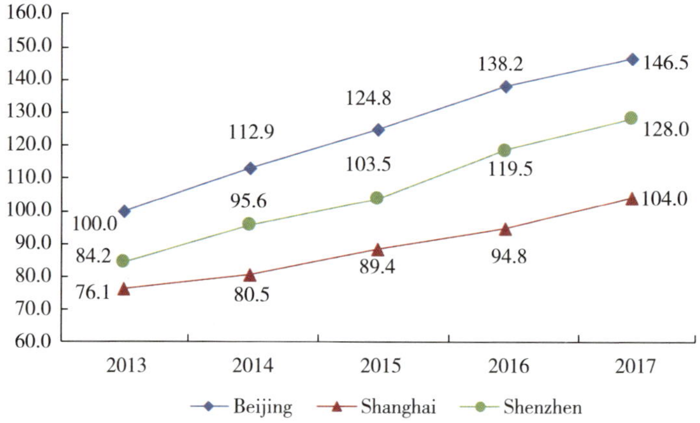

Figure 3 – 1   Development of the Comprehensive Index of Functions of

Beijing – Shanghai – Shenzhen Center of Science and

Technology Innovation (2013 – 2017)

2. The Five Major Functional Indexes Have Their Own Characteristics

(1) From the Perspective of Agglomeration Function, Beijing Has a Strong Resource Endowment

From the perspective of the five major functional indexes, Beijing has always maintained a leading position in the agglomeration function index. This advantage is still expanding, which is closely related to Beijing's highly intensive technological innovation resources of central universities and research institutes.

In 2017, the Beijing – Shanghai – Shenzhen agglomeration function index reached 128. 7, 71. 4 and 50. 6 respectively. There is a clear gap between Shanghai – Shenzhen and Beijing. Beijing is 57. 3 higher than Shanghai and 78. 1 higher than Shenzhen, which has an absolute advantage. From 2013 to 2017, Beijing's leading edge has become more and more obvious. The cumulative increase of the three places' indexes is 28. 7, 17. 4 and 7. 0 respectively. To be more specific, Beijing's advantage lied in the highly – concentrated resources of high – end instrument and equipment research and development personnel and universities. Shanghai had certain advantages over Shenzhen in high – end instruments and equipment. Shenzhen lead Shanghai in terms of R&D personnel strength. The agglomeration function of the science and technology innovation center is highly correlated with the innate resource endowment. Thus, Beijing's resource advantages are unmatched by other cities and cannot be surpassed in the short term.

(2) From the Perspective of Innovation Function, Beijing Has Double High Input and Output

High levels of resource agglomeration will inevitably lead to large – scale, high – quality innovation outputs. Beijing has fully utilized and exploited the favorable conditions of scientific and technological resources and has also shown strong advantages in terms of technological innovation output.

In 2017, the Beijing – Shanghai – Shenzhen innovation function index reached 165. 2, 66. 6 and 63. 5 respectively. Beijing was higher than Shanghai and Shenzhen by 98. 6 and 101. 7 respectively. From 2013 to 2017, Beijing's advantages continued to expand. The cumulative growth of the three places' indexes was 65. 2, 20. 2 and 23. 1 respectively.

From the perspective of innovation investment, Beijing gathered high – level scientists. The number of highly cited scientists ranked first in the country for a long time. The investment of Beijing in basic research was also at the national leading position. In the developed provinces and cities, its scale of investment and the proportion of R&D funds in the whole society ranked first. From the perspective of innovation output, Beijing's knowledge innovation output represented by papers and technological innovation output represented by invention patents were rich in achievements. The number of SCI papers and the number of 10000 people invented patent ownership ranked first in the country.

(3) From the Perspective of Driving Function, Shenzhen Keeps Leading

In 2017, the Shenzhen Driving Function Index reached 184.1 with an increase of 47.9 compared with 2013, which was higher than Beijing and Shanghai by 56.7 and 29.7 respectively. The Shanghai Driving Function Index was 154.4, 27.0 higher than Beijing. From the perspective of development trends, Beijing, Shanghai and Shenzhen were both showing growth momentum. The gap between Beijing, Shanghai and Shenzhen was expanding while the gap between Beijing and Shanghai was basically stable.

Based on the analysis of driving factors, high – tech manufacturing is a strong driving force for Shenzhen's development. The employment of high – tech manufacturing had grown rapidly. In 2017, the number of employed people in high – tech manufacturing accounted for 77.0% of high – end industries. Meanwhile, Shenzhen had obvious advantage of product innovation. From 2013 to 2017, the sales revenue of new products increased by 15.7% annually. In 2017, it reached 1.2 trillion yuan, 2.9 times that of Beijing and 1.2 times that of Shanghai. Knowledge – intensive service industry was an important driving force for Beijing's driving development. The number of employed people in the knowledge – intensive service industry grew at an average annual rate of 7.8%. In 2017, it accounted for more than 90% of the total number of employed people in the high – end industry.

（4）From the Perspective of Radiation Function, the Driving Effect of Beijing is Outstanding

As a national science and technology innovation center, Beijing is the source of knowledge and technology in China. While supporting its own development, Beijing shoulders the heavy responsibility of driving national development. In 2017, Beijing's radiation function index reached 116. 9, ranking first, with a cumulative increase of 16. 9, which was higher than Shanghai and Shenzhen by 21. 9 and 36. 6 respectively. The advantage of Beijing's radiation function lied in the overflow of knowledge and the overall scale of output technology. By investing in high – tech enterprises in different places to achieve the leading role of technological innovation of other regions, Shanghai's advantage lied in its strong industrial radiation capability. For Shenzhen, its advantage lied in highly active intellectual property transfer activities represented by patents.

In addition, from the perspective of radiation area, Beijing, Shanghai and Shenzhen have the following characteristics:

Beijing's "enclave model": Beijing is showing the characteristics of driving the whole country. Meanwhile, the key radiation areas are characterized by "enclave mode". **From the perspective of the co – authored papers**, the three provinces with the largest number of co – authored papers in Beijing in 2017 were Jiangsu, Shandong, and Guangdong, all of which were more than 2000 times, accounting for 35. 5% of the total number of the top 10 provinces and cities. **From the perspective of patent transfer**, the two provinces with the most transfer of patents in Beijing in 2017 were Jiangsu and Guangdong, both of which were more than 400, accounting for 38.1% of the total number of the top 10 provinces and cities. **From the perspective of corporate investment**, the top 10 provinces invested by Beijing are involved in the eastern, central, western and northeastern regions, with Hunan and Shanghai accounting for the most, accounting for 25.3% and 12.0% respectively, a total of 37.3%. Tianjin and Hebei, which belong to the Beijing – Tianjin – Hebei economic circle, also entered the top 10, which in total accounted for 16.3% of the total investment. **From the perspective of technology trading**, the total turnover of technology contracts in Beijing to other provinces and cities in 2017 was 232.73 billion yuan, of which the largest are Guangdong and Sichuan provinces, respectively 302.0 and 27.93 billion yuan, accounting for one quarter of the total amount, 13.0% and 12.0% of the turnover of the provinces and cities respectively.

Shanghai's "neighborhood model": **From the perspective of the co – authored papers**, in 2017, among the co – authored provinces for the Shanghai papers, Jiangsu and Zhejiang were among the top three. The number of co – author times was more than 2000, accounting for the top 10 35.0% of the total number of provinces and cities. **From the perspective of patent transfer**, in the transfer of patent provinces and cities in Shanghai in 2017, Jiangsu and Zhejiang ranked first and third respectively, with more than 800 and 400 respectively, accounting for 47.7% of the total number of provinces and cities in the number of patent transfers. **From the perspective of corporate investment**, Shanghai is dominated by the Yangtze River Economic Belt, accounting for 48.5% of the provinces along the route. Among them, Jiangsu and Zhejiang, which are located in the Yangtze River Delta Economic Circle, are among the top 5, accounting for 34.3%. Jiangsu is 26.7%, occupying the first place. **From the perspective of venture capital investment**, the total investment amount of Shanghai VC/PE investment institutions in Jiangsu, Zhejiang and Anhui provinces reached 23.35 billion yuan in 2017. The three provinces of Jiangsu, Zhejiang and Anhui all entered the top ten provinces and cities in Shanghai VC/PE investment, which fully reflects the radiation – driven effect of Shanghai science and technology finance on the Yangtze River Delta.

Shenzhen's "targeting model": **From the perspective of patent transfer**, the provinces and cities with the most patents transferred from Shenzhen to Guangdong in 2017 were Jiangsu, with more than 400 patents. The number of patent transfers accounted for 22.7% of the top 10 provinces and cities. The provinces and cities all has under 250 patents. **From the perspective of corporate investment**, Shenzhen's investment area is very concentrated. Beijing is absolutely leading in the market with nearly 2/3 share. It is the most popular investment area for Shenzhen enterprises. **From the perspective of technology trading**, in 2017, the technical transaction volume between Shenzhen and Shanghai surpassed the transaction volume of Guangdong Province (except Shenzhen), becoming the No.1 region, with 451 contracts and technical transaction volume of 12.797 billion yuan, accounting for 56.9% of the amount of technology transactions exported to the field.

(5) From the Perspective of Dominant Function, Shenzhen Has a High Starting Point and Fast Growth

Shenzhen's dominant function index has obvious leading edge, mainly due to the international development of Shenzhen enterprises, focusing on the global intellectual property layout, especially for companies such as Huawei, ZTE and Tencent.

The dominant function index of Shenzhen started from 125.1 in 2013 and reached 261.6 in 2017, which was higher than Beijing and Shanghai by 67.5 and 128.7 respectively. The cumulative increase in the past five years was 136.5. For Beijing and Shanghai, it was 94.1 and 62.2 respectively. From the gap between these three cities, the gap between Beijing and Shanghai and Shenzhen was generally expanding.

From the perspective of the path to achieve the dominant function, Beijing, Shanghai and Shenzhen have the following characteristics:

Firstly, Beijing, focusing on central enterprises, makes innovative strategies internationally. The central enterprises in Beijing are an important carrier of the capital's scientific and technological innovation and have contributed an important force to Beijing's construction of a national science and technology innovation center. In 2017, among the list of the Beijing enterprises selected as the top 2500 global R&D companies, the top 10 companies except Baidu and Lenovo were central enterprises. Besides, the total R&D expenditure of these 8 central enterprises accounted for 47.9% of the total 2500 enterprises in Beijing. At the same time, central enterprises had occupied some of the international technological high – tech points in areas with high technological content such as high – speed rail, UHV and smart grid, and had gained a leading position in the world's technological development trend.

Secondly, Shanghai's the main focus of strengthening global resource allocation is developing export – oriented innovation economy. As the seat of the first free trade zone in the Chinese mainland, Shanghai has long benefited from the export – oriented economy and has significant characteristics of high import and export commodities, as well as high international technology revenue. In 2017, Shanghai's exports of high – tech products accounted for 48. 6% of total merchandise exports, which were 5. 8% and 5. 2% higher than Beijing and Shenzhen respectively. Shanghai achieved international revenue of technology of USMYM15. 62 billion in 2017, 1. 8 and 2. 6 times that of Beijing and Shenzhen respectively.

Thirdly, Shenzhen achieved global intellectual property layout with PCT. Shenzhen's dominant function index has a high starting point and rapid growth. Its primary driving factor is the rapid growth of PCT patent applications. In 2017, the number of PCT patent applications reached 20457, accounting for 41. 9% of the total number of PCT applications nationwide. The average annual growth rate was 19. 4% from 2013 to 2017. The number of PCT applications put forward by Huawei alone reached 4024, which is close to 80% of Beijing's total applications. It was 1. 9 times the total amount of that of Shanghai.

3. Main Conclusion

The results of empirical evaluation show that the functions of the Beijing, Shanghai and Shenzhen science and technology innovation centers are constantly developing and upgrading. The comprehensive indexes of the functions of innovation center of science and technology witness a relatively large growth. From the function comprehensive indexes, Beijing ranked first. In the past two years, the gap between Shanghai, Shenzhen and Beijing had remained basically stable. The five major function indexes highlight the different strengths and weaknesses and development models of the three cities:

Beijing's agglomeration function, innovation function and radiation function rank first. Its dominant function index ranks second while its driving function index ranks third, presenting the technology – driven development model led by colleges and universities. Beijing has obvious advantages in congenital endowment and is rich in both college and university resources and technological achievements. Besides, as the most concentrated area of science and technology innovation resources in the country as well as a source of knowledge and technology in the country, Beijing continues to export knowledge and technological achievements to all parts of the country, forming a pattern that radiates across and leads the country, shouldering the important mission   as a national technological innovation center and reflecting the characteristics as a capital. However, Beijing still has a short board in terms of driving functions and dominant functions. Its industrial development momentum and global innovation influence need to be further improved.

Shanghai's four functional indexes of agglomeration, innovation, drive and radiation rank second. Its dominant function index is the third, showing a mixed economic development model that coexists with traditional industries and high – tech industries (new economies). Shanghai's overall development is relatively balanced, with a relatively good coordination. The dominant function is the focus of improvement. Among them, Shanghai is superior to Shenzhen but inferior to Beijing in terms of high – end instruments and scientific research institutions. In terms of innovation function, Shanghai is superior to Shenzhen but inferior to Beijing in terms of high – level scientists, basic research funding and high – level paper output. In terms of driving functions, Shanghai is superior to Beijing but inferior to Shenzhen in terms of capital productivity and new product output. In terms of radiation function, Shanghai's industrial radiation capability has obvious advantages, driving its radiation function indicator to continue to grow steadily. In terms of dominant function, Shanghai has advantages in both high – tech product export and technology international revenue. It is worth noting that the transformation of Shanghai's traditional industries has heavier mission and the momentum of high – tech development still needs to be improved. The intellectual property leadership represented by the PCT is the focus of efforts.

The driving and dominant function indexes of Shenzhen rank first. The three indexes of agglomeration function, original function and radiation function rank third, presenting an innovative development model characterized by high – tech industries (new economy). The rapid development of the Shenzhen driving function index is mainly due to the continuous improvement of labor productivity and the economic benefits brought by the output of new products. In terms of industrial development, the structure of the manufacturing industry has also been continuously optimized and improved while the proportion of high – tech products has continued to grow. The key factor for the leadership of the dominant function is the rapid development of its global patent layout, especially the leading role of anchor companies such as Huawei and ZTE. Shenzhen's high – tech development momentum is strong, traditional industry transformation tasks are not heavy and industrial development is extroverted. However, the lack of scientific and technological resources and the need to further enhance the surrounding radiation are issues that deserve attention.

Chapter IV

Evaluation of Agglomeration Function

The agglomeration function brings together resources for technological innovation, including talent, capital, R&D and service organizations, etc. It enables cities to achieve the "collection, aggregation and fusion" of global high – end innovation resources, which is the key to forming a good innovation ecosystem and the bedrock for building a science and technology innovation center.

1. Overall Situation

The agglomeration function index is focused on four indicators—talent, finance, materials and institution. Judging from the results of evaluation, Beijing has an absolute leading edge in terms of human resources in science and technology, R&D expenditure, high – end scientific research equipment and the number of universities. Besides, the R&D funding in Shanghai and Shenzhen have been growing steadily. Shenzhen, especially, has certain advantages, leveling up with Beijing in terms of investments on R&D personnel, even surpassing it in 2015.

When it comes to the specific index, Beijing ranks first, followed by Shanghai and Shenzhen. From 2013 to 2017, Beijing agglomeration function index increased from 100 to 128.7 (an accumulated increase of 28.7), while Shanghai index increased by 17.3, and Shenzhen 7.0.

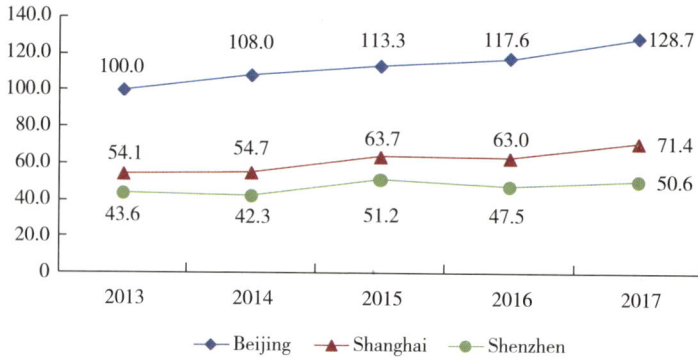

Figure. 4 – 1   Development Trends of Agglomeration Function Index in

Beijing – Shanghai – Shenzhen (2013 – 2017)

2. Detailed Analysis

(1) Beijing R&D Personnel Lead in Scale and Strength

It is widely recognized that personnel is the root of innovation activities, the source of competition, the key to transformation, and the drive of motivation for a country or region. Thus, R&D personnel is one of the most important human resources for innovation, referring to those involved in the research, management and support of research and experimental development projects, including project team members, administrators in science and technology, and direct assistants for project activities. The number of R&D personnel of 10000 employees is the indicator of the status of innovative human resources relative to the scale of employment.

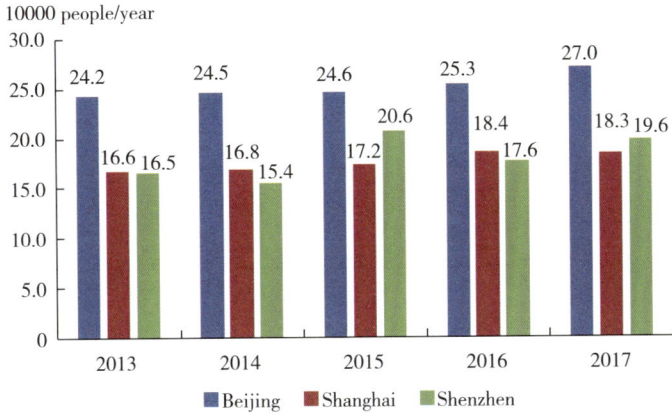

Figure 4 – 2   The Development Trends of the Total Number of R&D Personnel

in Beijing – Shanghai – Shenzhen（2013 – 2017）

In terms of the total number of R&D personnel, Beijing has been dominating Shanghai and Shenzhen in the past five years. In 2017, Beijing owns 270000 R&D personnel, while Shenzhen ranked second with 196000 people, and Shanghai 183000. From the growth of R&D personnel, Beijing's average annual growth rate was 2.7% in the past five years, Shanghai 2.6%, and Shenzhen 4.4%.

Concerning the number of R&D personnel of 10000 employees, Beijing and Shenzhen have been close rivals in the past five years, and they are leading alternately over Shanghai. As for the average annual growth rate, Beijing reached 4.3%, Shanghai 2.0%, and Shenzhen 3.2%. Beijing has maintained relatively rapid growth in human resources of scientific and technological innovation. Therefore, such abundant resources lay a good foundation for its further scientific and technological innovation activities.

Person/year/10000 People

Figure 4 – 3   The Number of R&D Personnel of 10000 Employees

in Beijing – Shanghai – Shenzhen（2013 – 2017）

（2）Beijing Remains High on R&D Funding Intensity

The proportion of R&D funding in the whole society to the GDP of the region is an internationally common indicator of innovation investment and can better evaluate the technological innovation capability of a region. The R&D funding intensity in Beijing has always remained the first in the country. It has been stable at over 5.5% since 2013 and reached 5.64% in 2017, 1.3% higher than Shenzhen and 1.64% higher than Shanghai. Seeing the development from 2013 to 2017, the intensity of Beijing R&D expenditures has shown a downward trend, while Shanghai and Shenzhen have steadily increased. In recent years, Shanghai has been focusing on the construction of science and technology innovation center, as well as on resources planning. In 2017, R&D expenditure ranked sixth in the country, with an average annual growth rate of 11.6%. Shenzhen continued to exert its strength

in innovation, increasing R&D funding, with an average annual rate of 14.5%.

Figure 4 – 4　The Proportion of R&D Expenditures in

Beijing – Shanghai – Shenzhen to GDP of the Region（2013 – 2017）

（3）Beijing is Resourceful in High – end Instruments and E-quipment

It is commonly known that the number of high – end instruments and equip-

ment reflects the conditions of scientific materials possessed by scientific research-

ers. The richer the conditions are, the more innovative results can be produced,

and the more likely can innovation enthusiasm of researchers be stimulated. There

are many central universities such as the Chinese Academy of Sciences, Peking U-

niversity, and Tsinghua University in Beijing, offering the city with unique science

and technology resources. In the past five years, Beijing has clearly led Shanghai and Shenzhen in terms of number of high – end instruments and equipment, with a steady upward trend. In 2017, there were 795 sets of high – end instruments and equipment in Beijing, 1.9 and 18.9 times of Shanghai and Shenzhen respectively.

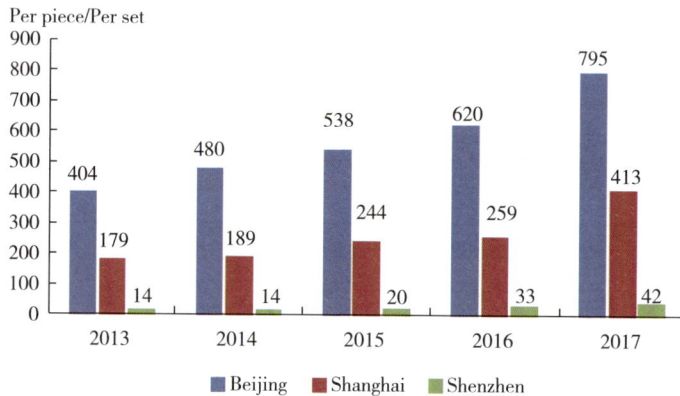

Figure 4 – 5　The Number of Beijing – Shanghai – Shenzhen High – end

Instruments and Equipment (2013 – 2017)

(4) Beijing Owns Clusters of Scientific Research Institutions

Scientific research institutions and universities are an important part of China's innovation system, bearing heavy responsibility for scientific research. The number of them can also reflect the degree of regional scientific research resources. During 2013 – 2017, the number in Beijing was the highest among three, remaining at more than 460, over twice that of Shanghai and over 25 times that of Shenzhen. Shanghai ranked second, basically maintaining around 200. Shenzhen came at the last, with a large gap, but this kind of resource advantage is the result of long –

term accumulation, and it is difficult to break through in the short term.

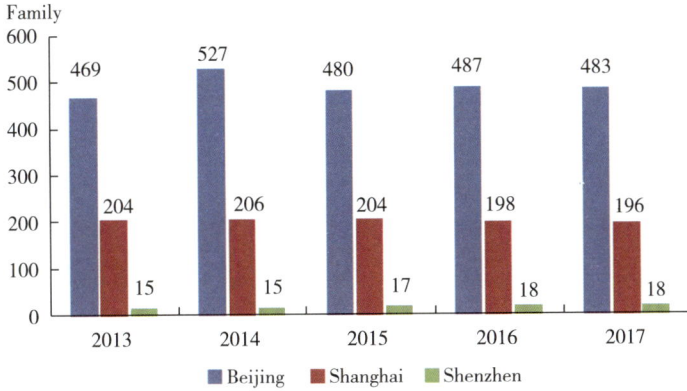

Figure 4 – 6 The Number of Scientific Research Institutions and Universities

in Beijing – Shanghai – Shenzhen (2013 – 2017)

3. Summary

Through the above analysis, in terms of agglomeration function, Beijing has an absolute advantage and is always in a leading position. Shanghai and Shenzhen also have their own characteristics.

Firstly, Beijing's advantages in agglomeration function are related to its special location. The cluster of a large number of central universities has brought unparalleled resource advantages, making Beijing rich in personnel, finance and materials, and equipping it with abundant technological resources, together with comparatively advanced personnel and capital intensity. It is worth noting that the number of R&D personnel of 10000 employees is gradually decreasing and may even be overtaken. In the current fierce competition among cities, attention should not only be paid to high – end personnel in the world, but also to grass – root R&D personnel.

Secondly, Shanghai ranks second only to Beijing in terms of the number of high – end instruments and equipment and the number of universities, thus having certain advantages over Shenzhen. Nevertheless, in terms of R&D personnel intensity and R&D funding intensity, Shanghai is counted as the last, adding its decreasing number of R&D personnel of 10000 employees in recent two years, there is still room for improvement compared with Shenzhen and Beijing.

Lastly, Shenzhen owns higher R&D investment per capita and R&D personnel intensity than Shanghai, competes closely with Beijing in the number of R&D personnel of 10000 employees and has a comparative advantage. It is second only to Beijing in terms of R&D funding intensity. In recent years, Shenzhen has been continuously progressing in innovation, and its R&D funding has continued to climb, with an average annual growth rate higher than Beijing and Shanghai. However, with weak technological background, there is still a big gap in the number of high – end instruments and equipment and the number of universities in Shenzhen, comparing with the other two cities.

Chapter V

Evaluation of Innovation Function

The innovation function is the overall ability of regional science and technology original innovation, the basis for enhancing the supply of innovation – driven source, and the core of global competition in science and technology. It not only marks the strength of the original innovation ability of a country and region, but also is the driving force for sustainable development of international metropolis.

1. Overall Situation

The indicators of innovation function focus on original input, knowledge innovation, and technological innovation, etc. The evaluation results show that Beijing possesses strong advantages in all the above aspects. With the construction of the National Science and Technology Innovation Center, Beijing is consolidating its status as the original source of innovation. From 2013 to 2017, Beijing innovation function index rose from 100 to 165. 2, an increase of 65. 2. The original innovation capacity of the Beijing Science and Technology Innovation Center has been greatly improved in the past five years.

Among evaluation results of the three, Beijing's innovation function ranks first, with a remarkable leading edge. From 2013 to 2017, the gap between their innovation function indexes gradually widened, and the difference compared to

Shanghai and Shenzhen in 2017 reached 98. 6 and 101. 7 respectively.

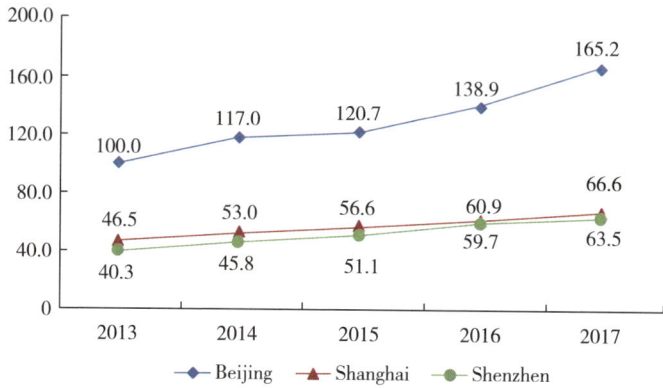

Figure 5 – 1   The Development Trend of Beijing – Shanghai – Shenzhen

Innovation Function Index (2013 – 2017)

2. Detailed Analysis

(1) Beijing Has Obvious Advantage on the Number of Highly Cited Scientists

Generally speaking, being listed as "Global Highly Cited Scientists" means that the scholars have world – class influence in their research fields, and their research results have contributed greatly to the development of this field. In recent years, Beijing has taken the lead in introducing and nurturing high – end personnel and actively encouraging original innovative personnel. From 2013 to 2017, the number of highly cited scientists in Beijing remained 12.3% per year. In 2017, it reached 94, 7.2 times that of Shanghai and 23.5 times that of Shenzhen.

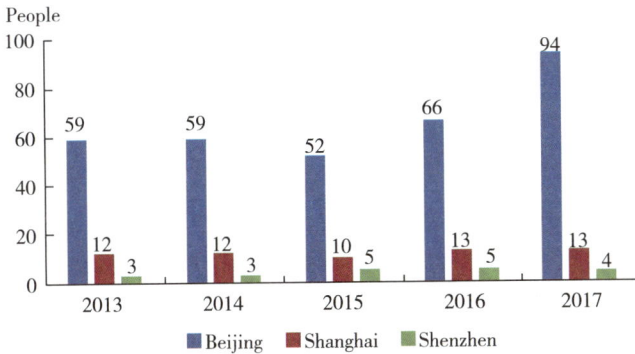

Figure 5 – 2   The Number of Beijing – Shanghai – Shenzhen

Global Highly Cited Scientists（2013 – 2017）

Analyzing the selected list, the scientific research institutions with strong scientific research strength and the "Double First – rate" universities are the main supporters of global highly cited scientists. With the strong advantages of the Chinese Academy of Sciences, Peking University and Tsinghua University, Beijing has seen more highly cited scientists on the list. Although Fudan University and Shanghai Jiaotong University perform well, there is still a big gap compared with Beijing. Shenzhen relies heavily on "Non – double First – rate" universities such as Shenzhen University and Southern University of Science and Technology.

（2） Beijing Leads Shanghai and Shenzhen on Fundamental Research Investment

Fundamental research is the foundation of original innovation, and it is also the support of product and equipment upgrades, reflecting the advanced original innovation capacities. For instance, Beijing's expenditure on fundamental research maintained rapid growth, from 13. 72 billion yuan in 2013 to 23. 24 billion in 2017, an average annual increase of 14. 1% . Compared with Shanghai and Shenzhen, Beijing is the leader of the innovation chain. In 2017, Beijing's fundamental research expenditure was 2. 5 times that of Shanghai and 7. 6 times that of Shenzhen. The major original scientific and technological achievements formed by Beijing's fundamental research have played an important role in breaking through major cutting – edge technologies and enhancing independent innovation capabilities and have become the core strength of the country's original innovation.

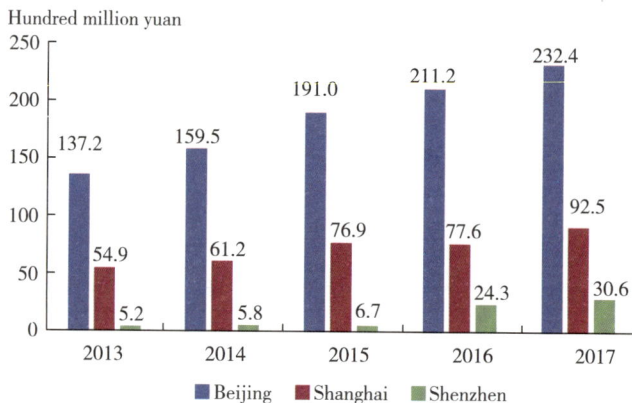

Figure 5 – 3   The Expenditure of Fundamental Research in

Beijing – Shanghai – Shenzhen （2013 – 2017）

The proportion of fundamental research funds to the total R&D expenditure of the whole society is an international indicator of original innovation capacity. From 2013 to 2017, Beijing's fundamental research funds accounted for 11.7% of the total R&D expenditure of the whole society, an increase of 3.1%. Far higher than the proportion of Shanghai and Shenzhen in the same period, Beijing has always been at the frontier of becoming an important source of national independent innovation and the main source of global original innovation.

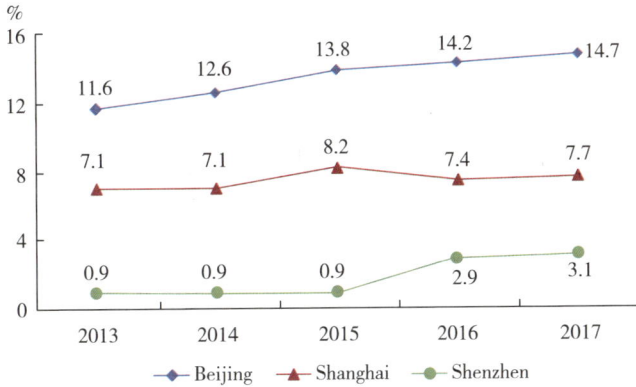

Figure 5 – 4   The Proportion of Fundamental Research Funds to Total R&D Expenditure in Beijing – Shanghai – Shenzhen (2013 – 2017)

(3) Beijing Ranks First in Knowledge Innovation

Knowledge innovation is the prerequisite of scientific and technological innovation. As a result of knowledge innovation, scientific papers serve as an important embodiment of the level and capability of original innovation. The number of papers included in SCI is an important indicator for measuring the level of knowledge innovation, which directly reflects original innovation capability. In 2017, Beijing published 52000 SCI papers, 1.9 times that of Shanghai and 17.3 times that of Shenzhen. During the period of 2013 to 2017, the annual average growth rate of SCI papers published in Beijing is 8.9%, 0.7% higher than Shanghai (8.2%) and 18.7% lower than Shenzhen (27.6%).

Figure 5 – 5   The Number of Published SCI Papers in

Beijing – Shanghai – Shenzhen (2013 – 2017)

(4) Beijing Witnesses Rapid Growth in Technological Innovation

The possession of patents is an important indicator of the strength of technological innovation and innovation development. In 2017, the number of patents in Beijing reached 205000, which is twice that of Shanghai and Shenzhen. From 2013 to 2017, the number of patents in Beijing increased by 24.6% annually,

4. 5% higher than Shanghai (20.1%) and 10.0% higher than Shenzhen (14.6%).

Ten thousand pieces

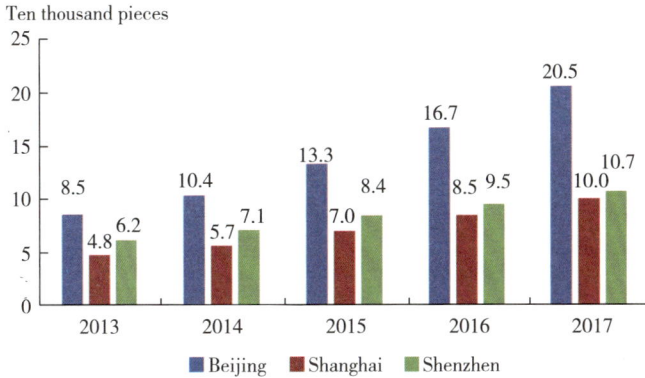

Figure 5 – 6   The Number of Patents in Beijing – Shanghai – Shenzhen

(2013 – 2017)

Patent ownership of 10000 people is an international common indicator, reflecting the technological innovation capability of a country or region. During 2013 to 2017, the number of patents in Beijing maintained rapid growth, with an average annual growth rate of 23.7%, exceeding Shanghai (20.0%) by 3.7% and Shenzhen (9.8%) by 13.9%. For the first time in 2017, it surpassed Shenzhen, reaching 94.6 pieces per 10000 people. Compared with Shanghai, the number of patents in Beijing has remained more than twice, and the gap has gradually widened.

Per piece/ten thousand people

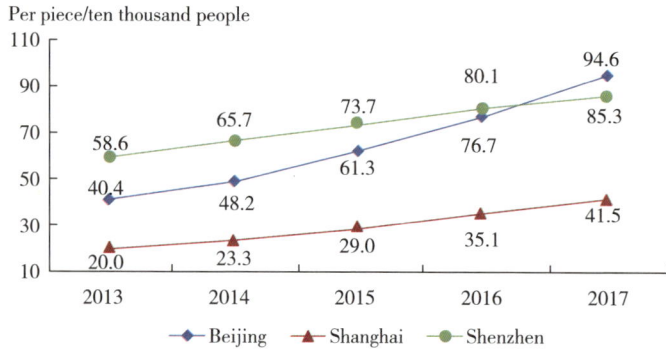

Figure 5 – 7   The Number of Patent Ownership of 10000 People in

Beijing – Shanghai – Shenzhen（2013 – 2017）

3. Summary

The above analysis shows that Beijing has a strong advantage in terms of origi-

nal function, while Shanghai and Shenzhen each have their own characteristics.

To begin with, Beijing leads Shanghai and Shenzhen significantly and with ev-

ident increasing trend in high – end personnel, fundamental research investment

and knowledge innovation output. Besides, Beijing exceeded Shenzhen in patent

ownership of 10000 people in 2017. Overall, it is the "vanguard" of original in-

vestment, knowledge innovation and technological innovation.

In comparison, Shanghai is in the middle in terms of high – end personnel,

fundamental research investment and knowledge innovation output. Its proportion of fundamental research funds to the total R&D expenditure of the whole society started to decline since 2015. Furthermore, its patent output falls way behind, thus, efforts are still needed in technological innovation. In the future, its potentials should be fully tapped, new development momentum should be stimulated and released, and regional technological innovation should be improved.

Finally, the number of patents in Shenzhen is the second highest. In contrast, it came the last in the number of global highly cited scientists, the investment in fundamental research, and the number of SCI papers. Although its proportion of fundamental research funds to the total R&D expenditure of the whole society started to pick up since 2015, it remained still the last. In the future, it is necessary to further increase original investment, to attract and nurture high – end personnel, so as to yield more original results of scientific research.

Chapter VI

Evaluation of Driving Function

Driven development is the core driving force for the development of science and technology innovation centers. It is the foundation for promoting the deep integration of science and technology and economic society. It is the foundation for realizing industrial transformation and driving social development. It is an important engine for achieving high – quality development. It is shaping more innovation – driven development, taking its first – mover advantage.

1. Overall Situation

Driving function is mainly reflected in the two aspects of industrial structure optimization and efficiency improvement. Judging from the evaluation results, Shenzhen has a leading edge in the past five years, with Shanghai and Beijing in the second and third places. In 2017, Shenzhen's driving function index was 184.1, higher than Beijing at 56.7 and Shanghai at 29.7. To be specific, Beijing owns advantage on the optimization and upgrading of the service industry structure. Shanghai's advantage lies in product innovation and capital productivity. Meanwhile, Shenzhen has shown advantages in product innovation efficiency, structure improvement of manufacturing industry, labor productivity and capital productivity.

From the perspective of development trends, the driving function index of three cities have shown steady growth, with Shenzhen ranking first. From 2013 to 2017, Shenzhen index increased by 47.9, higher than Beijing at 20.5 and Shanghai at 19.0. Overall, Beijing – Shenzhen, Shanghai – Shenzhen gaps have expanded year by year, while the gap between Beijing and Shanghai remains basically stable.

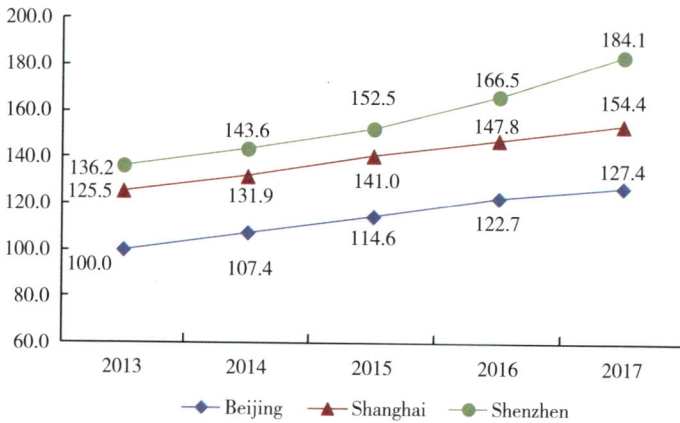

Figure 6 – 1   The Development Trend of Beijing – Shanghai – Shenzhen

Driving Function Index (2013 – 2017)

2. Detailed Analysis

(1) Beijing Has Great Potentials in the Development of High – end Industries

High – end industries include knowledge – intensive service industries and high – tech manufacturing industries characterized by high – tech content and high added value, featuring industrial structure improvement in both manufacturing and service industries. The employment condition of high – end industry in Beijing has obvious advantages in terms of scale and growth rate. In 2017, the number of employed people in high – end industry in Beijing reached 3. 17 million, 1. 6 times that of Shanghai and 1. 5 times that of Shenzhen. From 2013 to 2017, its average annual growth rate of high – end industry employment was 6. 7% , 4. 9% higher than Shanghai and 3. 7% higher than Shenzhen. Looking at the reason behind, the rapid growth of high – end industry personnel provides strong support for the development of high – end industries.

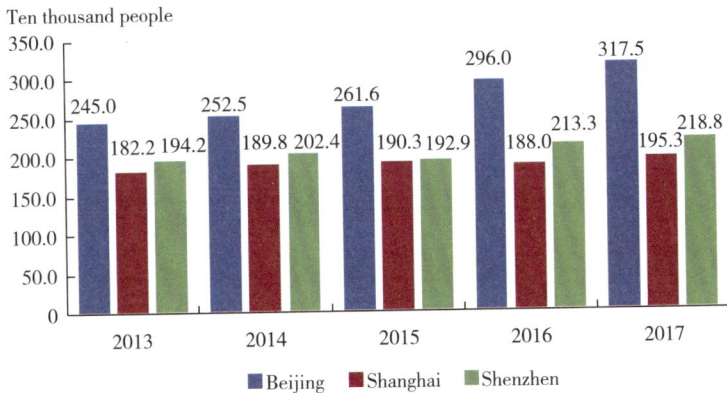

Figure 6 – 2 The Number of Employed People in High – end Industries in Beijing – Shanghai – Shenzhen (2013 – 2017)

The proportion of employed people in high – end industries to employed people in the whole society can reflect the optimization of industrial structure and the impact of innovation on employment. After surpassing Shenzhen in 2015, Beijing has been leading Shanghai and Shenzhen in the past two years. In 2017, the number reached 25.5% with an increase of 7.0% compared with the situation in 2013 in which one out of four employees was in high – end industries, 11.3% higher than Shanghai and 2.3% higher than Shenzhen.

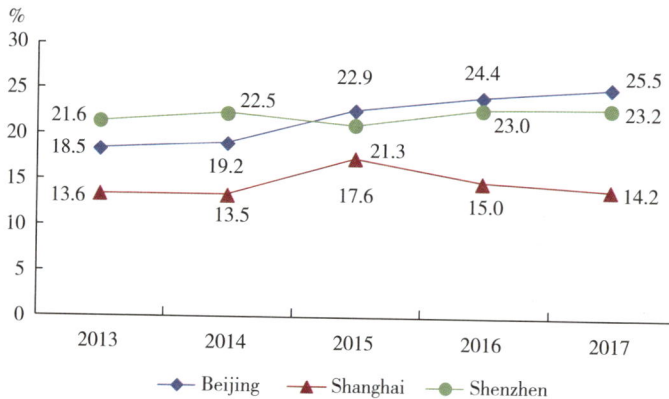

Figure 6 – 3   The Proportion of Employed People in High – end Industries

to Employed People in the Whole Society in Beijing – Shanghai –

Shenzhen (2013 – 2017)

(2) Shenzhen Remains No. 1 in Product Innovation Output

New products are one of the most direct outputs of innovation and a reflection of the degree activity of innovation activities in the market. The increase in sales revenue of new products reflects the continuous optimization of the supply – side structure and the improvement of the quality of economic development. From 2013 to 2017, the sales revenue of new products in Shenzhen increased by 15.7% annually, reaching 1.2 trillion yuan in 2017, 2.9 times that of Beijing and 1.2 times that of Shanghai. The sales revenue of new products in Shanghai and Beijing ranks second and third respectively. In contrast, the development of new products in Beijing is relatively slow, this, the annual sales growth is only 2.9%.

Hundred million yuan

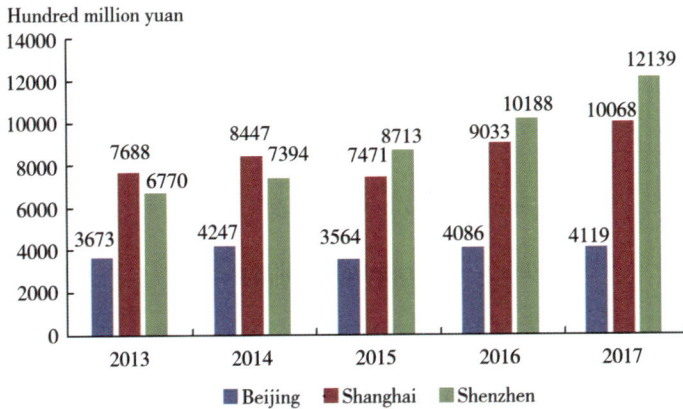

Figure 6 – 4   The Sales Revenue of New Products in Beijing –

Shanghai – Shenzhen (2013 – 2017)

(3) Shenzhen Excels in Labor Productivity

Labor productivity is a comprehensive indicator for evaluating the quality of economic development. It reflects the transformation of economic development mode from the perspective of labor saving and is calculated as the ratio of total production to the number of employed people. It is shown that Shenzhen has outstanding performance in labor productivity, with 238000 yuan per person in 2017, higher than

Beijing's 13000 yuan per person and Shanghai's 15000 yuan per person. Unfortunately, Beijing has been lagging behind Shenzhen in labor productivity, with noticeably decreasing growth rate in the past two years.

Ten thousand yuan/per Person

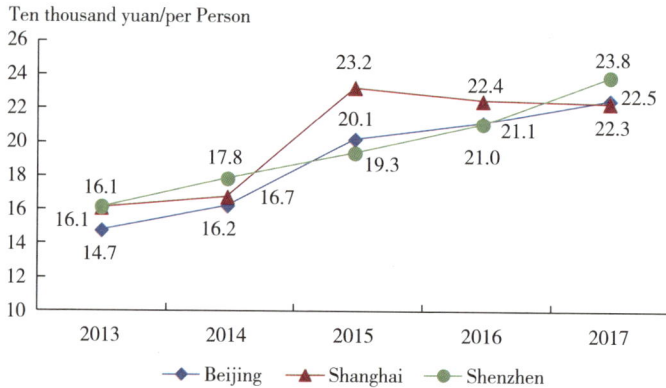

Figure 6 – 5   The Comparison of Labor Productivity in

Beijing – Shanghai – Shenzhen（2013 – 2017）

（4） Shenzhen Stays on the Top of Capital Productivity

Capital productivity reflects the relationship between capital input and economic output and is an indicator for measuring capital productivity per unit. Although Shenzhen's capital productivity has shown a downward trend as a whole, it has always maintained a leading position. In 2017, the number hit 4200 yuan per 10000 yuan, higher than Beijing's 400 yuan per 10000 yuan and Shanghai's 200 yuan per 10000 yuan. As for the other two cities, Shanghai's capital productivity has shown a slight increase, while Beijing has been growing slowly, leaving a certain gap compared with Shanghai and Shenzhen.

Ten thousand yuan/Ten thousand yuan

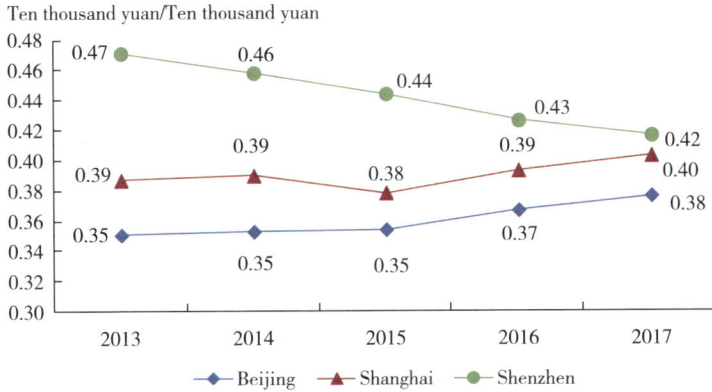

Figure 6 – 6   The Comparison of Capital Productivity in

Beijing – Shanghai – Shenzhen (2013 – 2017)

■ 3. Summary

To sum up, in terms of driving function, Beijing, Shanghai and Shenzhen have advantages in different aspects.

To start with, Beijing has a comparative advantage in developing high – end industries dominated by services. Its scale of employment, the growth rate of high – end industries, and the proportion of employed people in high – end industries to employed people in the whole society are higher than those of Shanghai and Shenzhen, demonstrating rather substantial potential for development. However, efforts still need to be made in both new product development and capital productivity.

Overall, Shanghai is in the middle in terms of product innovation and capital productivity. There is still a gap for Shanghai when comparing with Beijing Shenzhen in high – end industries and labor productivity, adding decreasing proportion of employed people in high – end industries to employed people in the whole society, needing further improvement.

Lastly, it is suggested that Shenzhen performs exceptionally in high – end industries and development efficiency, has shown strong advantages in product innovation, labor and capital productivity. It exceeds Beijing and Shanghai in sales revenue of new product, labor productivity and capital productivity. Nevertheless, with a downward trend in capital productivity (diminishing marginal productivity), there is still much room for improvement in the development of high – end service industry.

Chapter VII

Evaluation of Radiation Function

Radiation function refers to the driving force and comprehensive influence of regional science and technology innovation on the development of surrounding areas or external areas. It radiates to the surrounding areas and other provinces, autonomous regions and even the whole world through technology, capital, talents, information, management, policies, etc. It is the important guarantee for maintaining interaction and the key for Science and Technology Innovation Center to demonstrate leadership role in the country and the world.

1. Overall Situation

Radiation function has three aspects: Knowledge spillovers, technology flows and industrial driving ability. From the evaluation results, in 2017, Beijing's radiation function index reached 116.9, ranking first, respectively, higher than Shanghai - 22.0 and Shenzhen - 36.6. From the perspective of index movement, the Beijing - Shanghai deep radiation function index showed an overall upward trend, with cumulative increases of 16.9, 11.3 and 4.4 in five years.

From the specific indicators, the three regions have their own advantages. The main advantage of Beijing's radiation function lies in knowledge spillover and the overall scale of output technology. Shanghai's advantage lies in its strong industrial driving ability. Shenzhen is good at highly active patent transfer activities.

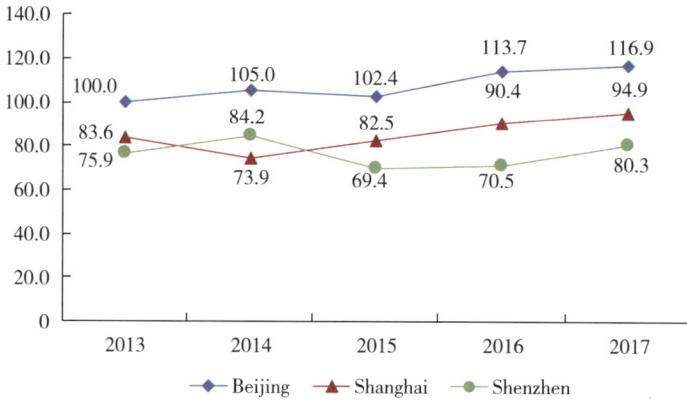

Figure 7 – 1   Development Trends of Beijing – Shanghai Deep

Radiation Function Index (2013 – 2017)

2. Detailed Analysis

(1) Knowledge Radiation Drive Effect of Beijing is Outstanding

The scientific papers of remote cooperation reflect the relationship between regional knowledge innovation and other regions, as important indicators for characterizing knowledge spillovers. From 2013 to 2017, the number of scientific papers in Beijing, Shanghai and Shenzhen has increased volatility, but the growth rate is subtle, with an average annual growth rate of 1.0% , 1.3% and 4.8%. In terms of scale, Beijing has extremely obvious advantage, always are more than three times that of Shanghai and more than 11 times that of Shenzhen. Thus, its spillover effect of knowledge innovation is outstanding.

Cooperation frequency Per Paper

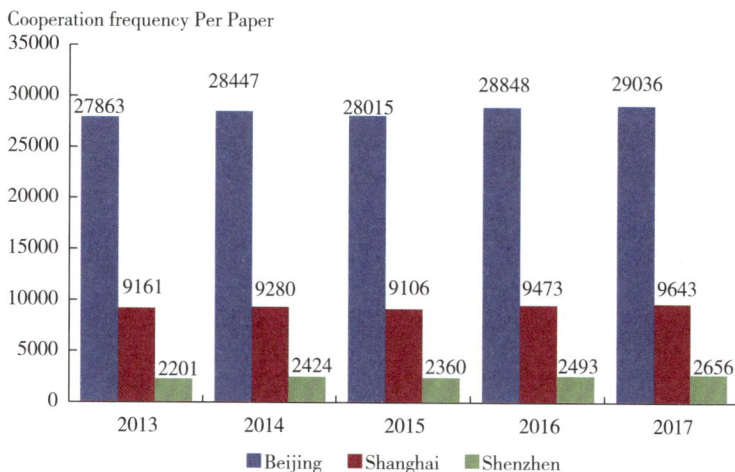

Figure 7 – 2   The Number of Co – authored Scientific Papers in Different Places in Beijing – Shanghai – Shenzhen (2013 – 2017)

(2) The Overall Scale of Beijing's Technology Radiation is Powerful

In addition, the turnover of technology transactions is another indicator reflecting the flow of technology. It can be divided into three parts: Flow to the local, flow to the nonlocal places and flow to the abroad. The flow of technology transactions to the nonlocal places reflects the driving effect of a city in the radiation of other parts of the country through technology transactions. As a national technology distributing center, Beijing's technology transaction turnover accounted for about one – third of the country's total turnover, and the proportion of outputs to other provinces and cities in China remained above half. From the output to off – site technology contract turnover, Beijing ranked first of the three cities in 2017 with a scale of more than 200 billion yuan, 5.4 and 6.6 times that of Shanghai and Shenzhen respectively.

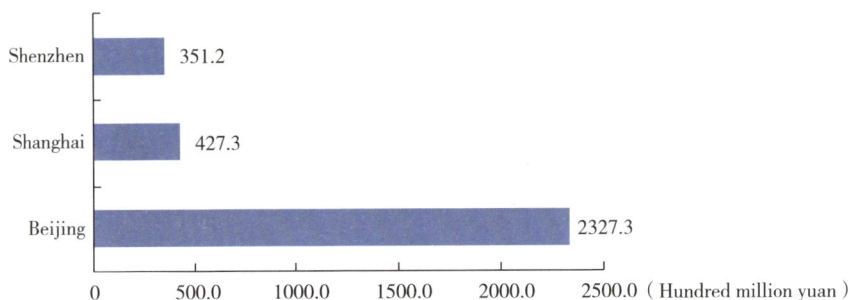

Figure 7 – 3   Output to Off – site Technology Contract Turnover in

Beijing – Shanghai – Shenzhen (2017)

(3) Patent Technology Spillover Effect of Shenzhen is Strong

The number of patents transferred from different places reflects the link of technological innovation between regions, as an important indicator of technological mobility. In the past five years, the number of patents transferred from Beijing, Shanghai and Shenzhen was increasing, with an average annual growth rate of 13.2%, 17.7% and 56.2%. In terms of scale, Beijing has always been relatively leading in 2013 – 2015, but its advantages are not obvious. In 2016 and 2017, Shenzhen achieved leap – forward growth, especially in 2017, which increased by 1. 2 times, and jumped to the top of the three places, namely Beijing and Shanghai 1. 9 and 1. 8 times.

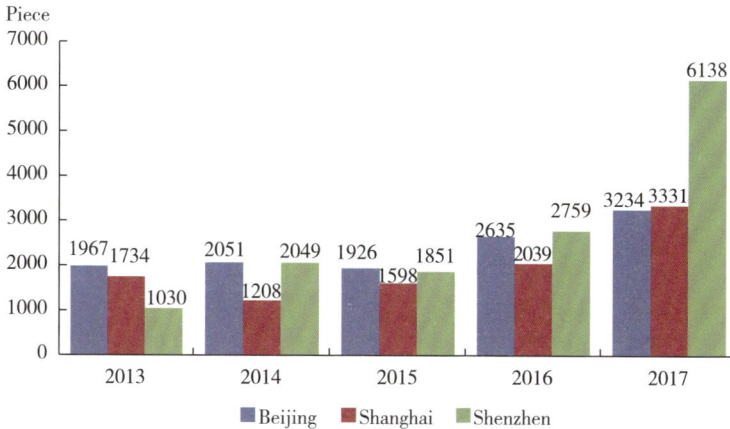

Figure 7 – 4　The Number of Patents Transferred from Different Places in

Beijing – Shanghai – Shenzhen（2013 – 2017）

Looking at the proportion of the number of patents transferred from different places to total number of transferred patents, Beijing's indicator is a dynamic trend, with no significant growth overall. In 2017, it only increased by 0. 6 percentage points compared with 2013. The rapid development of Shenzhen mainly started from the rapid upward trend from 2016, with an increase of 9. 4 and 12. 7 percentage points in 2016 and 2017 respectively. Shanghai showed a trend of first dropping and then rising, with a cumulative increase of 3. 1 percentage points.

（4）The Driving Effect of Shanghai's Industrial Radiation is Obvious

The off – site investment of enterprises can be regarded as an important way for regional industries to form radiation driving effect towards other regions. The investment in high – tech enterprises can reflect the role of industrial capital in driving other regions' technological innovation. The proportion of high – tech enterprises in different places invested by local enterprises of Shanghai has shown a steady growth trend, and has remained above 50% , much higher than Shenzhen and Beijing. This indicator of Shenzhen has continued to decline year by year, with a cumulative decline of 14.8 percentage points in five years, but is always higher than Beijing while Beijing has remained basically stable, between 30% and 40%.

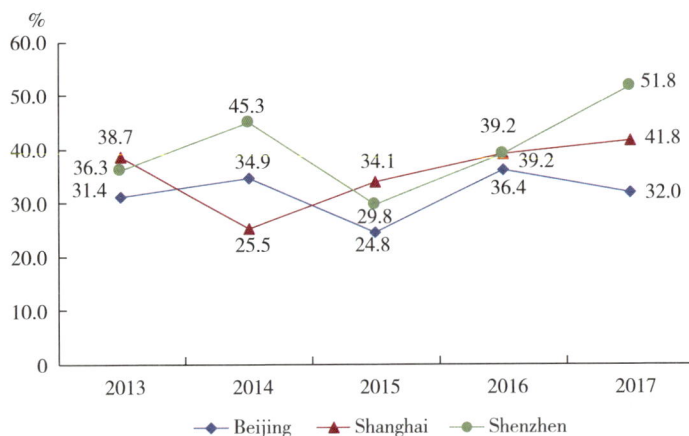

Figure 7 – 5   The Proportion of Patents Transferred from Different Places to the Total Number of Transferred Patents in Beijing – Shanghai – Shenzhen（2013 – 2017）

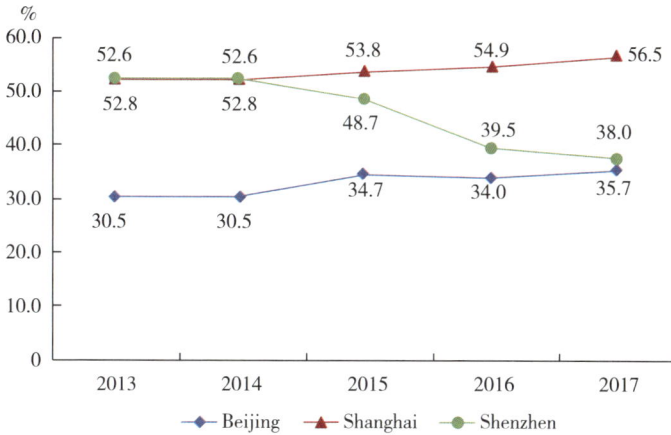

Figure 7 – 6   The Proportion of High – tech Enterprises in Different Places Invested

by Local Enterprises in Beijing – Shanghai – Shenzhen (2013 – 2017)

Note: The data for 2014 is used to replace the vacancy of data for 2013.

3. Summary

Through the above analysis, in terms of radiation function, Beijing, Shanghai and Shenzhen all showed stable growth trends with different characteristics.

As a national knowledge innovation source, Beijing has an overwhelming ad – vantage in knowledge spillover, which is closely related to the innate resource en – dowment advantage gathered by colleges and universities. The large – scale technol – ogy market is also a strong support for Beijing to exert its radiation function. The num – ber of technical contracts and turnover per year flowing to other provinces and cities nationwide are 30000 and 150 billion yuan respectively. Beijing still has a large room for improvement in patent transfer and industrial radiation, especially patent transfer. The number of patents in Beijing is in a leading position in the country while a large amount of patent resources have yet to be explored.

Shanghai's advantage lies in its strong industrial radiation capability. By invest – ing in high – tech enterprises in different places, it can achieve the driving effect of technological innovation for other regions. The proportion of high – tech enterprises in different places invested by local enterprises has always remained above 50%. Shanghai's knowledge radiation is less than Beijing's, and patent radia – tion is not as good as Shenzhen. While driving its own development, Shanghai should pay attention to improve the spillover effects of knowledge and technology.

For Shenzhen, its advantage lies in the high active intellectual property transfer activities represented by patents, as well as efficient patent technology spillover, which is closely related to the characteristics of its leading innovation. Its knowledge radiation is much lower than Beijing and Shanghai. Knowledge spillover is its obvious shortcoming, in line with the conclusions of the aforementioned agglomeration function and original function evaluation. Universities in Shenzhen are in lack of knowledge innovation entities, but the accumulation and exertion of such resources are the result of a long period of accumulation, which needs time and efforts.

Chapter VIII

Evaluation of Dominant Function

The dominant function is an important manifestation of a region grasping key resources and mastering strategic initiative. It is the core support for directing global innovation, occupying the high end of the value chain and the innovation chain, as well as enhancing the innovative influence in the international arena, as well as the ultimate embodiment of the function of the Science and Technology Innovation Center.

1. Overall Situation

The indicators of dominant function focus on high – tech investment companies, high – tech products, international revenue of technology and intellectual property rights. Judging from the evaluation results, Shenzhen has an absolute advantage. In the past five years, the dominant function has remained the first among Beijing, Shanghai and Shenzhen. In 2017, the index reached 261.6, which was 1.3 times that of Beijing and 2.0 times that of Shanghai. Beijing's dominant function is better than Shanghai, and next to Shenzhen, with a rising overall trend reaching 194.1 in 2017, nearly double the number in 2013. Shanghai's dominant functional index ranked third, and growth is relatively slow, only 132.9 in 2017.

To be more specific, Beijing's advantages are mainly concentrated in the number of high – tech investment companies; Shanghai's advantages are in high –

tech products and technology international income; Shenzhen's advantages are in

international patents.

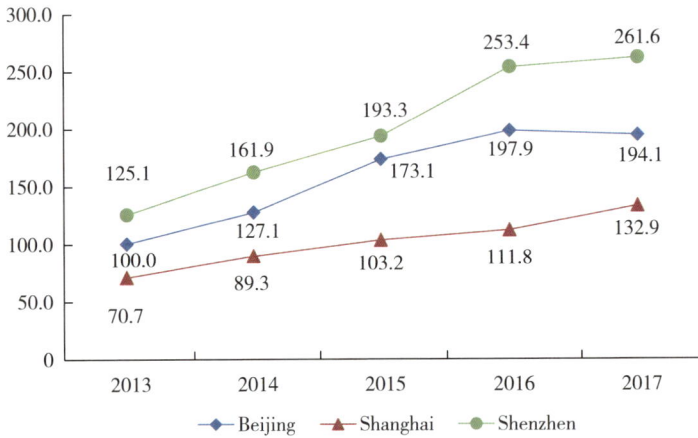

Figure 8 – 1　Development Trends of Dominant Function Index in

Beijing – Shanghai – Shenzhen（2013 – 2017）

2. Detailed Analysis

（1）The Large Number of High – tech R&D Enterprises in Beijing

The top 2500 companies in the global R&D investment reflect the global distribution of technology companies with high – tech investment. For a long time, high – tech companies in the United States have been the global leader and promoter of innovation, but with the continuous development of China's economy, Chinese company has also continuously strengthened its R&D investment. In particular, the number of high – tech R&D investment enterprises in the three science and technology innovation centers – Beijing, Shanghai and Shenzhen has continuously increased, and it has gradually formed a strong potential in the global enterprise innovation pattern.

From the evaluation results, Beijing has obvious advantages. In 2017, 81 enterprises were short – listed, 2 times that of Shenzhen and Shanghai while Shenzhen and Shanghai are basically the same. Judging from the changes in the past five years, the number of enterprises in Beijing, Shanghai and Shenzhen has maintained a high growth rate. Among them, Beijing had only 18 in 2013, and it has grown rapidly to 81 in 2017, with a cumulative increase of 3. 5 times in five years. Shanghai and Shenzhen go hand in hand, with a cumulative increase of 3. 4 times and 4. 1 times in five years.

It is worth noting that most of the companies on the list from Beijing are large central enterprises such as Petro China, China Construction Group, China Railway Group, and CRRC Group. However, Shenzhen was dominated by private enterprises that the total R&D funds of Huawei, ZTE and Tencent is 105. 49 billion yuan, which was 1. 7 times of the total R&D expenditure of all enterprises in Beijing.

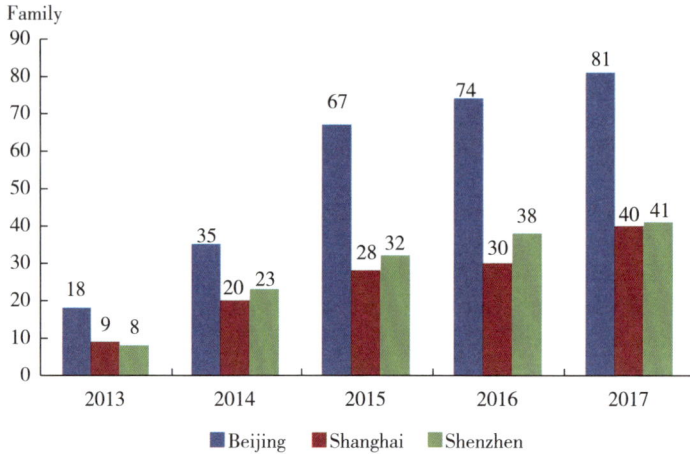

Figure 8 – 2   Development Trends of the Number of Top 2500 Companies in Global R&D Investment in Beijing – Shanghai – Shenzhen (2013 – 2017)

(2) Continuous optimization of Shanghai's Commodity Export Structure

The proportion of exports of high – tech products to merchandise exports reflects the international competitiveness of high – tech products and the leading ability of products. Shenzhen has an absolute advantage from the perspective of the total export volume of high – tech products. In 2017, the export volume of high – tech products reached 114. 57 billion US dollars, 10. 1 times that of Beijing and 1. 4 times that of Shanghai. Judging from the changes in the past five years, the export of high – tech products in Beijing, Shanghai and Shenzhen has shrunk in an all – round way, and all are in a downward trend. Among them, the export volume of high – tech products in Shenzhen dropped significantly. The data of 2017 was only 68. 1% of 2013. In 2017, the export value of high – tech products in Shanghai

was 84. 53 billion US dollars, 7. 5 times that of Beijing, which declined slightly in

the past 5 years, just taking up 95. 3% of 2013; Beijing's high – tech products

export value was the smallest with the fastest decline that the data in 2017 was only

55. 6% of 2013.

Hundred million dollars

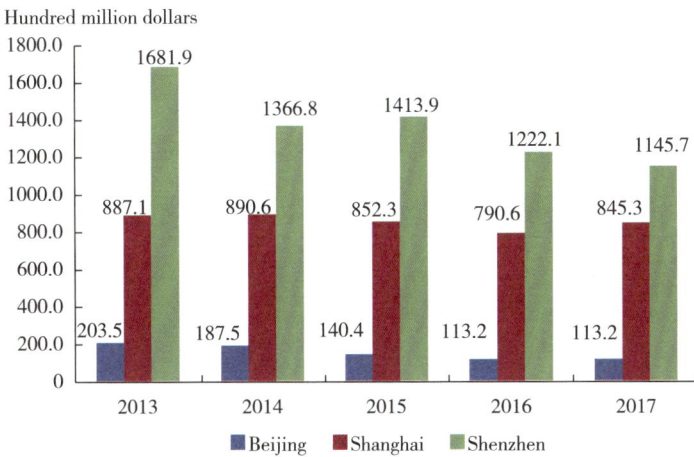

Figure 8 – 3   Development Trends of the Exports of High – tech Products in

Beijing – Shanghai – Shenzhen（2013 – 2017）

From the perspective of the proportion of exports of high – tech products to

merchandise exports, Shanghai has 48. 6% in 2017, which is 5. 8 and 5. 2 per-

centage points higher than Beijing and Shenzhen respectively. The export value of

high – tech products in Shenzhen accounted for 43. 4% of the total export value of

goods, ranking second, 0. 6 percentage points higher than Beijing. Beijing was on-

ly 42. 8% , ranking the last. From the perspective of changes in the past five years, Shanghai had a slow growth trend, with a cumulative growth of 1.6 percentage points in five years; Shenzhen was in a volatile downward trend, with a cumulative decline of 8.2 percentage points in five years; Beijing was rapidly declining year by year, with a cumulative decline of 18.5 percentage points in five years.

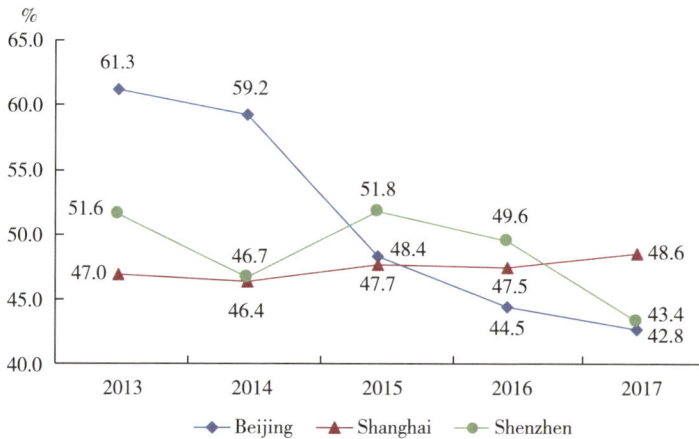

Figure 8 – 4   Development Trends of the Proportion of Export Value of

High – tech Products to the Volume of Merchandise Exports in Beijing –

Shanghai – Shenzhen (2013 – 2017)

(3) The Scale of International Income of Technology in Shanghai is Prominent

International technology trade is an important means of international technology resource allocation, application and dissemination of technical knowledge. The technological international income status of a country (region) reflects the country's (regional) international scientific and economic strength and economic status.

From the perspective of international revenue of technology, Shanghai has a significant advantage. In 2017, the international revenue of technology was 15.62 billion US dollars, 1.8 times that of Beijing and 2.6 times that of Shenzhen. Beijing was 8.49 billion US dollars, 1.4 times that of Shenzhen. From the changes in the past five years, Shanghai has steadily increased year by year. In 2017, it was 1.3 times that of 2013, with an average annual growth rate of 5.9%. Beijing showed a significant downward trend. The data of 2017 was only 86.6% of 2013. Shenzhen rose first and then fell. In 2013 – 2015, it grew steadily year by year, and then fell slightly in the next two years.

Hundred million dollars

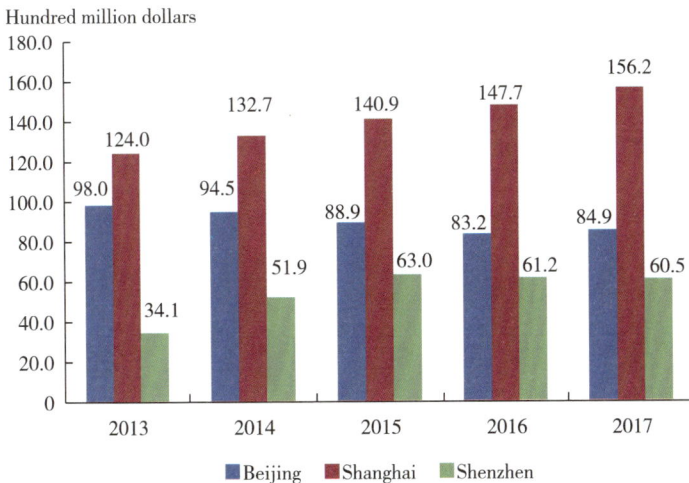

Figure 8 – 5   Development Trends of International Revenue of Technology in Beijing – Shanghai – Shenzhen (2013 – 2017)

（4） The Dominant Ability of Intellectual Property Rights in Shenzhen is Outstanding

The PCT applications are internationally accepted indicators that reflect the quality of innovation output and the international competitiveness of a country or region, as well as the leading ability of intellectual property and the competitiveness of international innovation output.

Through the analysis of the data, Shenzhen's advantage is obvious. In 2017, the number of PCT applications reached 20457, which was 4.0 times that of Beijing and 9.7 times that of Shanghai. The number of PCT fillings of a Huawei has reached 4024, nearly 80% of Beijing's total applications, which was 1.9 times that of Shanghai. Compared with Shanghai, the number of PCT applications in Beijing has an advantage, with 5069 in 2017, 2.4 times that of Shanghai. From the changes in the past five years, Beijing, Shanghai and Shenzhen have shown rapid growth. Among them, Shenzhen has doubled its PCT applications in five years, with an average annual growth rate of 19.4%; Beijing was also showing a growth trend that the applications in 2017 was 1.7 times in 2013, with an average annual growth rate of 14.2%; Shanghai had the fastest growth, and the data of 2017 was 2.4 times that of 2013 with the average annual growth rate of 24.1%.

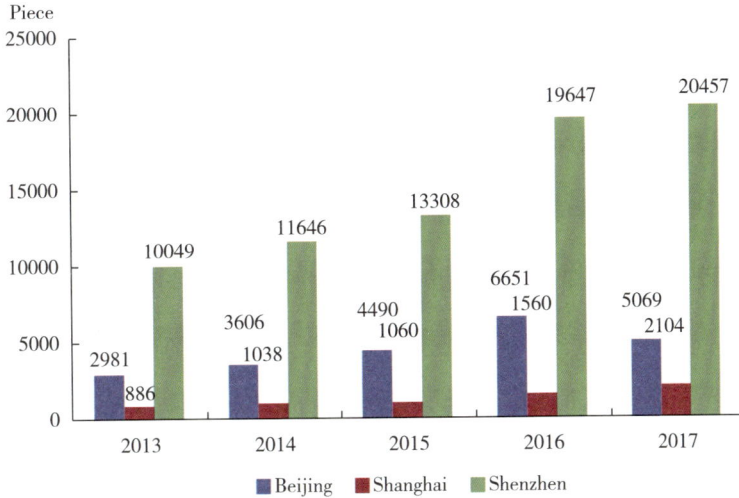

Figure 8 – 6   Development Trends in the Number of PCT Fillings in

Beijing – Shanghai – Shenzhen（2013 – 2017）

3. Summary

To summarize, in terms of dominant function, Beijing, Shanghai and Shen -

zhen all showed continuous growth with different characteristics from different lead-

ing aspects.

Firstly, the advantage of Beijing's dominant function lies in the large number

of high – tech R&D investment companies. The number of top 2500 companies in

the global R&D investment is much higher than that of Shanghai and Shenzhen,

but these enterprises are mainly central enterprises. Beijing's exports of high –

tech products and international revenues of technology are declining, and the interna – tional patent layout still needs to be strengthened.

Secondly, Shanghai's advantages of dominant function are mainly reflected in the export of high – tech products and international revenue of technology. In 2017, its proportion of the exports of high – tech products to merchandise exports is much higher than that of Beijing and Shenzhen, as well as the international revenue of technology. The quality of Shanghai's export – oriented economy continues to im – prove. There is still much room for improvement in both high – tech investment companies and international patent layout.

Thirdly, Shenzhen has obvious advantages of international patents. The num – ber of PCT patent applications is much higher than that of Beijing and Shanghai. The leading technology companies represented by Huawei are particularly outstand – ing. Shenzhen's high R&D investment enterprises still need to work hard on the overall quantity, commodity export structure and international revenue of technology.

Indicator Interpretation

(1) The number of R&D (Research and Development) personnel of 10000 employees. R&D personnel is one of the most important human resources for innovation. As the main indicator of the level of human resources, it refers to the personnel involved in the research, management and auxiliary work of research and experimental development projects, including project (subject) team members, science and technology administrative personnel and support personnel who directly provide services for project (problem) activities. The number of R&D personnel in 10000 employees is an indicator reflecting the status of innovative human resources relative to the scale of employment.

(2) R&D funding intensity. It means ratio of R&D expenditure to GDP, which are the most important and comprehensive indicators for measuring the intensity of science and technology financial input. When the per capita GDP reaches 3000 – 4000 US dollars in developed countries, the lowest level of it is 2.5%.

(3) The number of high – end instruments and equipments. High – end equipment refers to a single (set) scientific research equipment that is included in the asset management of a legal entity with an original value of 5 million yuan (including 5 million yuan). High – end instruments and equipments are the basic conditions for scientific research and technological innovation, and their application level is an important indicator to measure the level and potential of science and technology development of a country.

(4) The number of research institutions and universities. Scientific research

institutions refer to institutions engaged in scientific research activities that focus on basic scientific research and applied scientific research. Colleges and universities refer to ordinary higher education institutions. They are schools that are administered by the Ministry of Education or the provincial education administrative departments (including autonomous regions and municipalities directly under the Central Government). Scientific research institutions and universities are an important part of China's innovation system which bear the heavy responsibility of scientific research. The number of them can reflect the degree of regional intellectual resources.

(5) The number of highly cited scientists in the world. The global list of "highly cited scientists" is based on the latest data and advanced algorithms from the Clarivate. It analyzes and evaluates the papers in the field of natural and social sciences collected by SCI in the past ten years in 21 major discipline fields, and ranks the first 1% of the frequency of he – cited of the papers. The inclusion of the "Highly cited Scientists" list means that the scholar has world – class influence in his field of study, and his research results have contributed greatly to the development of the field.

(6) The proportion of basic research funding to R&D expenditure in the whole society. R&D can be divided into basic research, applied research and experimental development according to the type of activity. Basic research refers to experimental or theoretical work in order to obtain new knowledge of the basic principles of phenomena and observable facts (prompting the nature of objective things, the laws of motion, obtaining new discoveries and new disciplines), which

is not intended for any specific or specific application. The proportion of basic research funding to the total R&D expenditure of the whole society is an indicator that reflects the original innovation ability internationally.

(7) The number of SCI papers. Internationally, the SCI (Science Citation Index) database is commonly used to evaluate basic research results. It contains selected papers published in important scientific journals of various countries in the world, which is often referred to as "SCI papers".

(8) Patent ownership of 10000 people. The number of patents is an important indicator reflecting the output of science and technology activities in a country (region) while the number of invention patents is a more important indicator. The volume of invention patents reflects the stock of valid invention patents at a certain point of time.

(9) The proportion of employed people in high – end industries to employed people in the whole society. High – end industries, including knowledge – intensive services and high – tech manufacturing, respectively reflect the mid – to high – end industries of the secondary and tertiary industries. High – end industries frequently use high – tech, which is the main industry to absorb high – quality labor. The proportion of high – end industry employment personnel in the whole society reflects the proportion of high – skilled and high – quality talents in the whole society, as well as the optimization and upgrading of industrial structure.

(10) New product sales revenue. Product innovation activities are the most important innovation activities of enterprises. The output of new products is an important symbol to transform enterprise innovation activities into real productivity.

(11) Labor productivity. Labor productivity refers to the ratio of labor results created by workers in a certain period of time to their corresponding labor consumption. It is an indicator that reflects the transformation of economic development mode from the perspective of labor saving, and is the ratio of total production to the number of employed people.

(12) Capital productivity. It refers to the output created by unit capital in a certain period of time. This indicator measures the output capacity of unit capital. The higher the unit capital outputs, the higher the capital productivity can be. Capital productivity reflects the relationship between capital input and economic output meaning the ratio of GDP to capital investment.

(13) The number of co – authored scientific papers in different places. It reflects the relationship of knowledge innovation between one region and other regions, and is an important indicator for characterizing knowledge spillovers.

(14) Output to off – site technology contract turnover. The turnover of technology transactions is an important indicator reflecting the flow of technology. It is divided into three parts: Flow to the local, flow to the field and flow to the foreign countries. The turnover of the technology transaction to the field is an important indicator and a reflection of the driving effect of a region to other regions in the country through technology transfer.

(15) The proportion of the number of patents transferred from different places to the total number of transferred patents. It reflects the link between technological innovation of one region and other regions, as an important indicator of technology flow. It also reflects the extent of technology flow across regions.

(16) The proportion of high – tech enterprises in different places invested by local enterprises. It refers to the proportion of high – tech enterprises registered in the field among high – tech enterprises invested by enterprises in other regions. This indicator can reflect that technological innovation can drive technological innovation in other regions.

(17) The number of top 2500 companies in the global R&D investment. The Joint Research Center of the European Commission's Science and Knowledge Services Agency publishes a list of top 2500 companies around the world in terms of R&D investment. The number of companies in the list can reflect the R&D status of a country or region around the world.

(18) The proportion of exports of high – tech products to merchandise exports. The exports of high – tech products is based on the data separated from the export of commodities according to the High – tech Product Catalogue of the General Administration of Customs, and is calculated according to the country of origin. It can reflect the international competitiveness of high – tech products.

(19) International revenue of technology. International technology trade is an important means of international technology resource allocation and application of technical knowledge. International revenue of technology mainly refers to the transfer of intellectual property rights such as patents, non – patent inventions, trademarks, R&D services and other technical services to other countries. The international revenue of technology status of a country (region) reflects the country's (regional) international scientific and technological strength and economic status.

(20) Number of PCT patent applications. The PCT international applications

are globally recognized as an important indicator for measuring the innovation capabilities of a country, region and enterprise, especially for international competitiveness. They are the primary measure for assessing intellectual property and patent competitiveness. Paying attention to PCT international patent applications is crucial to improving patent layout, acquiring more markets and winning greater economic benefits in the competition.

References

[1] JAFFE A B, TRAJTENBERG M, HENDERSON R. Geographic Localization of Knowledge Spillovers as Evidenced by Patent Citations [J]. The Quarterly Journal of Economics, 1993, 108 (3): 577 – 598.

[2] EC. European Innovation Scoreboard 2017 [R]. European Commission, 2017.

[3] OECD. Managing National Innovation Systems [R]. Paris: OECD, 1999.

[4] XUAN Zhaohui, ZHU Yingchun, LIU Huifeng, et al. National Innovation Index Report 2016 – 2017 [R]. Beijing: Science and Technology Literature Press, 2017.

[5] LIU Xielin. China's Regional Innovation Ability Evaluation Report. 2017 [R]. Beijing: Science and Technology Literature Press, 2017.

[6] 2thinknow. Innovation Cities™ Index 2016 – 2017 : Global [EB/OL]. 2017 – 02 – 22. http: //www. innovation – cities. com/innovation – cities – index – 2016 – 2017 – global/9774.

[7] DU Debin, HE Shunhui. The Connotation, Function and Organization of Global S&T Innovation Center [J]. Forum on Science and Technology in China, 2016 (2): 10 – 15.

[8] LIAO Mingzhong, HU Yubin. Evolution Characteristics and Enlightenment of International Science and Technology Innovation Center. [J]. Urban Insight, 2019 (3): 117 – 126.

［9］ HUANG Jing – jing, ZHANG Zhi – juan, LI Fu – qiang. Analysis of Global Science and Technology Innovation Center Evaluation and Suggestions for Beijing ［J］. Global Science, Technology and Economy Outlook, 2018, 33 (6): 56 – 63 + 70.

［10］ ZHANG Shiyun, WANG Jian, PANG Liyan, et al. Research and Evaluation of Functions of S&T Innovation Cente ［J］. WORLD SCI – TECH R&D, 2018, 40 (2): 61 – 70.